# Birth Out of Darkness

# Birth Out of Darkness

Bertrille Williams

# Birth Out of Darkness

Bertrille Williams

Birth Out of Darkness

Copyright © 2020 by Bertrille Williams.

All rights reserved. No part of this book may be reproduced or transmitted in any form or by any means, electronic or mechanical, including photocopying, recording, or by any information storage and retrieval system, without permission in writing from the copyright author, except for the use of brief quotations in a book review.

Library of Congress Cataloging-In-Publication Data

Name: Williams, Bertrille, author.
Title: Birth Out of Darkness / Bertrille Williams

Identifiers:
LCCN: 2020922777
ISBN: 978-1-970135-66-4 **Paperback**
    978-1-970135-67-1 **Hardcover**
    978-1-970135-68-8 **Ebook**

Published in the United States by Pen2Pad Ink Publishing
www.pen2padink.org.

Requests to publish work from this book or to contact the author should be sent to: buzbody52000@yahoo.com

Birth Out of Darkness

## Contents

| | |
|---|---|
| Dedication | 9 |
| Acknowledgements | 11 |
| Hey, Little Brown Girl! | 13 |
| Introduction | 15 |
| Embrace Your Darkness | 19 |
| **Chapter 1:** The Day Darkness Fell | 21 |
| Who Am I? | 27 |
| **Chapter 2:** Stolen Moments | 29 |
| There is A Seed In You | 42 |
| **Chapter 3:** There is A Seed In You | 44 |
| Thank You Son | 52 |
| **Chapter 4:** I Am Not My Decision | 54 |
| Take Back Your Keys | 63 |
| **Chapter 5:** The Promise | 65 |
| Baby, Just Breathe | 75 |
| **Chapter 6:** B.G. (Before Grace) | 78 |
| Your Grace | 85 |
| **Chapter 7:** Five Years of Grace | 86 |
| I'll Just Adjust My Crown | 100 |
| **Chapter 8:** Change of Plans | 102 |
| Victim's Cry to Victor's Shout | 111 |

*Chapter 9:* Get Up! ... 113
Utilize Your Gifts ... 122
*Chapter 10:* Birthing of a Ministry ... 124
Missing You ... 137
*Chapter 11:* A Place of Hurt and Pain ... 138
Keep Trying ... 143
*Chapter 12:* Here Comes The Flood ... 142
Beast Mode! ... 152
*Chapter 13:* Shift Your Position ... 154
Slay Queen Slay! ... 161
*Chapter 14:* Rising of a Phoenix ... 164
The Hands of my Ancestors ... 172
*Chapter 15:* Birth Out of Darkness ... 174

*For You*

My Beauty ... 180
Don't Come For Me! ... 182
The Quarantine Talent Show ... 184
Black Man Swag ... 187
You Got My Back? ... 189
Do You See Me? ... 191
Get Connected ... 193

## *Dedication*

I would like to dedicate this book to my Dad, **_Thurman Lofton._** To my greatest inspiration and hero in life. Thank you for giving me a strong foundation in God. Thank you for being a man of Faith, Love, and having a heart for people. Your legacy will live on within your children and God is going to do everything He promised you for your seed. I have been blessed beyond measure just because God allowed you to be my father, my Bishop, and my friend. Love and miss you Dad!

Birth Out of Darkness

*Acknowledgements*

I first want to thank God from which all inspiration and blessings flows. I want to thank my parents Thurman and Betty Lofton for giving me a firm foundation in God. You both have given me the blueprint on how to work hard, trust in God, and to make your dreams a reality.

To my husband Eric Williams and my two blessings from heaven: Terrell Lofton, Ryt'jus Williams, you are the reason I fight to be the best version of me.

To my siblings Amanda Jones, Michael Jones, Tony Jones, Sulene Deloatch, Thurman Lofton Jr, Nicole Lofton and Savaslas Lofton. Thank you for your prayers, Godly advice, and for always supporting me in everything I put my hands to do.

Thanks to the rest of my family, co-workers, and friends who listened to me throughout this whole process and pushed me to get it done. Thank you to every person, every event that aided in my darkness, birthing process, and for thinking I wouldn't rise out the ashes like a Phoenix. Thank you to everyone who trusted the Calling God placed on my life and those who allowed me to just be me.

Thank you for your continued prayers and I'm thanking God for lives that will be impacted by my life experiences. I love you all, and I look forward to seeing you at the top!

Special thanks to Latonia Cameron, Karen Buie, Tiffany Grier, Gwendolyn Jones for sowing a seed into God's ministry and cheering me on every step of the way.

Thank you to Laya Trotman and Angela Brown for making sure I stayed on task, met every deadline, and being my technical support.

Thank you to Comic Steve Brown, Quarantine Talent Show Family, Niva Brown for sharing your artistic gift along with Darian Chamblee, who saw the vision from the beginning and never let me forget it.

Thank you to Angela Chatman for obeying God and for being the key that opened the door of opportunity.

Last but not least, millions of thanks to Pen2Pad Ink Publishing. I couldn't have done any of this without you.

## Hey, Little Brown Girl!

Hey, little Brown girl.
Did you know the day you were born
God blessed this world with a special gift?
A gift as rare as a Unicorn.
A girl more beautiful than any Disney Princess.
Because of you,
God made the whole earth shift.
The earth had to make room for a little Brown girl like you
with a smile as bright as any star.
A brown girl who is brilliant, talented, and equipped with the ability to go so very far.

Hey, little Brown girl.
You are filled with hopes and dreams.
You can become our next Doctor,
Astronaut, Scientist, or President!
Child, you can become anything.

Hey, little Brown girl.
When you look in the mirror, always love the image you see.
Tell yourself every day:
I am strong,
I am powerful,

# Birth Out of Darkness

I am smart, and
I am blessed
just to be me.
Don't let anyone dim your light
or let them try and stop your shine.
Never compromise who you are,
Be confident.
Remember God made you,
and never be afraid to use your brilliant mind.

Hey, little Brown girl.
Always love the skin you're in.
Love the body God gave you
and your uniqueness is what makes you great.
When God created you,
He made you just the way you are.
He made you flawless and without a single mistake.

So for all the little Brown girls in this world:
Walk with your heads held high,
and always reach for the sky.
Don't ever let anyone put a cap on your ceiling.
Tell the world I'm phenomenal,
so there's no way you can pass me by.

## *Introduction*

I've always known that God had a plan for my life. I realized it for the first time around the age of five. I knew I was different, but to what magnitude I had no clue. So where do I start? Well, no better place to start than the beginning.

My mom always told me that I get my sensitive side from her because she cried a lot when she was pregnant. We never discussed in detail what was going on in her life that caused her to cry so much during that time. Maybe that's a conversation I need to have at a later date. Around the age of five, I recall being a dreamer. My dreams would have vivid colors, smells, and be full of imagery. I dreamed about angels, the coming of Christ, and the rapture. Can you imagine having those kinds of dreams at the age of five? I thought I was weird, and I often wondered if this was happening to any of my other siblings. So yes, I've always known I was special and that there was something peculiar about me.

I've heard several times throughout my life you have a book inside of you, you should tell your story, but I didn't receive it because my thoughts towards myself at the time was "Girl, don't nobody want to hear what you have to say." But God reminded me to look back over my life, the choices that I have made, and for me to recognize that people have always wanted to hear what I had to say. We all have a unique story to tell that can impact and influence someone if we just tap into it.

"You know what? You need to write your book." Comedian Steve Brown spoke those words to me on May 8, 2020. Why? Because I was walking inspiration. "Before you do anything else, you must write your book. Your time is now and people need to hear what you have to say." He continued. I kept hearing this over and over again.

I met comedian Steve Brown during the Covid-19 pandemic that hit the United States in January 2020. During that time, Steve started a "Quarantine Talent Show" on Instagram Live. I clicked on his live broadcast and noticed Steve was giving people a chance to display their gifts and their talents. One Sunday, I decided to showcase my talent. So I got my nerves together, sent a request to sing, and he picked me. I did the gospel song "I Won't Complain". After I finished, Steve asked "Uh...ma'am. Do you beat your kids? 'Cause the way you ended that song...I know somebody butt is red!" I laughed in relief from the song being over and Steve enjoying my performance.

I sang about two other times after that. During a couple of the songs, I noticed a few trolls in the comments, so I decided to write what I like to call "Clap Back Poetry". It's my 'artistic' way to handle bullies. This became my signature talent for the show. This is also how the conversation for the book came to be. So here we are. It was after our conversation that I heard a 'click' in my spirit.

Later that night, I prayed to God to give me the right words to say. To bless me with words that would impact this world and change someone's destiny while allowing me to be transparent with my story. Then I heard the title for the book: "Birth Out Of Darkness." The words leaped into my spirit immediately and I said to myself: YES! THAT'S IT!

Then I hit a dead-end. Nothing.

I realized I had to deal with some past hurts and unforgiveness first before I could allow the Holy Spirit to guide my pen. I had to deal with the brokenness that I had buried. God allowed me to see that when I started writing. He didn't want my story to be distorted. Instead, He wanted me to come from a place of victory and not a place of being a victim. So, I invite you to take a peek into my life's journey. I want to share with you some important small fragments of my life, how these experiences impacted who I am and the woman I have become. I pray that my small victories will encourage you, comfort you, uplift you, and challenge you to birth something out of your time of darkness.

## *Embrace Your Darkness*

Embrace your darkness. That's where regaining your control back begins. When you can trust the God that can grant you peace, love, forgiveness and power, there's no way your enemies can continue to win.

Darkness, if given the authority, can make you feel vulnerable, insecure and can leave you second guessing who you are. It's a constant tap on your shoulder reminding you of your failures, hurts, and scares.

But God says "No!" Let me remind you that I have placed my light deep within. Let me show you how I will illuminate and command all darkness inside you to come to an end. You see your darkness was not a form of punishment. It was never intended to make you throw in the towel, to give up, or cry out to God "Why did you bring me into the wilderness to die!"

It was created as a place of resurrection, a place for you to grow, to learn to live and to thrive. Let your darkness challenge you to become a warrior, a dreamer, and birth something great!

Embrace your darkness, take back your power, and know that with God on your side. It's never too late.

# Chapter 1

## *The Day the Darkness Fell*

My first critical shifting moment happened when I was seven years old. I had no idea that this event would affect and alter the next twenty-eight years of my life. I spent a lot of time at my grandmother's house. I loved going over there because she always had a way of making me feel like I was special. In my mind, I felt like I was one of my grandmother's favorites, but I can't say that my other siblings or cousins would agree. One day, I was playing outside with my older sister and my cousin. My Aunt Teresa was home visiting from out of state.

"Jessica! Tracy! Constance! Y'all get in here!" My aunt yelled.

"Did we do something?" We all asked at the same time. We felt like we were headed to the principal's office. My aunt sat us down *ccording to our age: my sister (who was the oldest), my cousin, and then myself.

She looked at my oldest sister with a smile on her face and said, "You are the pretty light-skinned one."

Then, she turned to my cousin and said, "You, Sweetie, are the pretty dark-skinned one."

She then looked at me and said, "But baby...you gone have to develop a personality because you're the ugly duckling." Keep in mind: I'm a seven-year-old child. Why would you, as an adult, speak those words into the life of a seven-year-old girl? I just sat there, replaying her words over and over again in my head: *What would possess you to do that? Why would you plant that kind of seed into my life?* It was at that moment that the darkness fell.

My sister and cousin went back outside as if everything was normal. I, however, just sat there thinking: *What am I supposed to do with this?* I couldn't understand why an adult, one of the people that is supposed to help protect me, would try to cause that kind of damage to a child's self-esteem.

In the next twenty-eight years of my life, I struggled with low self-esteem, body image problems, and depression while working overtime to develop this so-called "personality". While my aunt walked away feeling like she had given me some words of advice that would help me, she left me empty thinking. How do I get someone to like me as an ugly duckling. Will I ever become a beautiful swan?

This moment impacted my life, shaped my destiny, and mapped out the road to becoming who I am today. Because I had allowed those words to take root and gain power in my life at the age of seven, they became the driving force and the foundation for me. Who would have thought that these simple words would map out how I chose a mate in a relationship, how I would see myself, and how it would shape my personality altogether? We have all heard the saying "sticks and stones may break my bones, but words would never hurt me". That is a lie. Words can hurt you, shape who you are, and kill you spiritually.

Later on in life, I discovered that she had her version of the darkness she was dealing with. Everyone has a root cause of their inner struggles. If we are not wise, we will project our insecurities onto innocent people. I was an innocent child who was not allowed to discover who I was because someone decided to make that decision for me. I went from being a clueless seven-year-old to having an ugly duckling complex. This is how the darkness fell, and this is my journey of how I clawed my way back to the light while becoming a beautiful swan.

Always Remember...

- Brokenness is an event and not a condition. God can take what was meant to break you and use it to change you.

- God will hide you to protect you and not kill you.

- God will heal you, but you must be willing to let Him.

God,

I want to pray for every young person who has been damaged by the words of an adult. I pray for every ugly duckling and for every child that has been broken and whose destiny has been altered all because someone decided to project their hurt and life experience on an innocent child.

God, place a hedge of protection around every little boy and little girl who will struggle for years as an adult and will walk with a burden that does not belong to them.

God, break every curse word spoken over their lives and replace it with the Word of God that everything that you created was good.

God, cover them with love, mercy and grace.

God, allow them to forgive those who clearly didn't know better. Even if they did, let them understand the damage they have caused. Cover each child by the Blood of the Lamb and grant them the ability to recover.

God, place mentors in their lives who will pray for them. Teach them how to overcome and show them how to take the darkness that fell over their lives and birth something great from it.

God, allow the darkness to be consumed by the light of your only begotten son Jesus Christ.

We speak joy, love, restoration and peace over each of your children.

In Jesus Name,

Amen

## *Who am I?*

When I look in the mirror, who or what do I see?
At times, I don't know.
Because there are so many faces staring back at me.
I see a woman who is always professional and exudes excellence at her job.
A Wife, a Warrior for everyone else, a Worker at home, a Wonderful friend to many, and a Willing Mom.
So many masks to choose from.
Which one will I be?
Out of all my many choices, which one is Me?
One mask for my strength, my wisdom, my faith, and a veil called love which we continuously seek.
Of all the choices I've been given, there's none.
No mask for the times when I want to be weak.
So, I'll continue to exchange my mask out because that's what I was taught.
Don't show the real me: what a false sense of life I have bought.
I'm tired of all the false images.
It's time we all get real.
Time for the real me to finally be revealed.
The real me? Now, who or what will that be?

When I see her, can I embrace her or believe that she is truly me?

Can I accept her for who she is and let God fix her? That's the only way she can be saved.

For I must remember, it was God that declared in Psalm 139: 14, "I will praise you, for I am fearfully and wonderfully made."

So the next time you look in the mirror and don't like what you see

Or you wish you were your sister,

Remember, she's not who you were called and created to be.

Just remember the rest of verse 14:

"Marvelous are your works and that my soul knows very well".

For your reflection in the mirror is where your true story dwells.

## Chapter 2

### *Stolen Moments*

When the darkness fell, I ingested my Aunt's words every day for breakfast, lunch, and dinner. Although I was a quiet child growing up, I cried a lot. I was sensitive about everything. I took pride in pleasing my parents, I didn't like getting into trouble, and I tried my best to not be on the receiving end of any kind of discipline at school or home.

I grew up in a two-parent home with parents who were God-fearing, and I was what they called a "PK" (preacher's kid). My parents made sure we had good manners, knew the difference between right from wrong, and worked hard for whatever we wanted. We are a family of eight children: four boys and four girls. Love was in the house, and we all had different personalities. One of my nicknames was "Ms. Strawberry Shortcake Can't Do No Wrong" because I didn't like getting into trouble. Little did they know how those words added to my darkness. I wasn't trying to be a perfect kid. I just didn't like getting in trouble.

My time in school would make the real Ms. Shortcake proud. I was labeled a teacher's pet. I worked hard in class, and I tried to make as many friends as I could remember so I could develop a personality. I ran for class president, I was voted "Most Friendly" one year, and then I was voted the class clown the next year. I joined the drama club, sang in the school choir, and played basketball and softball. I was well on my way to having this personality I so-called "needed".

My personality mask was set, but it could not protect me from everything. Around 14 and 15, I studied with a friend of mine, Trina. Trina had an older brother, Patrick, who stayed in trouble. I heard that Patrick spent some time in jail, he was in a gang, and he looked mean. If I'm honest, I was terrified of him. Whenever I went to her house, I never talked to him. I didn't make eye contact with him. I tried my best to be invisible because the way he looked at me was just creepy.

One day Trina asked me to come over to her house to study. I got permission from my parents to ride the school bus to her house. On this particular day, she missed the school bus. When I arrived at her house, Trina was not there yet, and Patrick answered the door. "Hi. Um...Is Trina home?" I asked.

"She ain't here," He started with a smirk, "But you can come in and wait for her." Everything in my gut told me to wait outside, but since her younger brother was home too, I thought it would be ok. Her brother allowed me to wait in her room until she came home from school, so I started my homework. At some point, I needed to use the bathroom. I asked him if he could show me where the bathroom was, and he did. A nagging feeling punched me repeatedly in my stomach. Something wasn't right.

When I returned from the bathroom, Patrick was sitting on the bed in Trina's room. Now the way the room was set up, I had to pass by him to get my things, and I also had to pass by him to leave. I started to gather my books because I felt uncomfortable, and I just wanted to go home. I didn't realize that Patrick had closed the door behind me when I came back into the room.

"I think I'm going to go. Tell Trina I came by." I said as I gathered by stuff.

"Why you in a rush?" He asked. Then, he started moving toward me.

"Patrick...what are you doing? I...I just want to leave." I asked.

"That ain't happenin' right now." He started moving towards me and covered my mouth. I tried to push away and head to the door, but he was too strong. He threw me on the bed. "Keep your mouth shut." He said. The door creaked open, and his little brother walked in "Pat...what you doing?" He asked.

"Shut up and close the door!" Patrick screamed. I tried to wiggle to get out of his grip, but I couldn't. Then, my skirt went up. Then, something was painfully inserted into me like a huge ice pick being shoved in my skin. This constant insert continued for who knows how long. I just prayed for it to be over. When he finished, he left the room. I remember feeling coldness and wetness all over the bed. Then, I realized it was blood. I thought I was dying. When he came back in the room, he threw towels at me.

"Wipe yourself off." He demanded. I felt numb like I had left my body. What just happened? How did this happen? Where was Trina? Why didn't his little brother help me? I had a sweater in my bookbag, so I tied it around my waist and left the room. As I was walking down the hallway, I heard Trina screaming at Patrick.

"What did you do to Constance?"

"Man, I didn't do nothing. Gone about yo' business!" He lied. When I came around the corner, she ran up to me. "You ok?" She asked.

"I...I just want to go home." I said. We walked past her brother who was sitting on the sofa like nothing happened.

"Sis...I'm so sorry." Trina said.

"Just...just take me to my Aunt Jackie." I answered quietly. She hugged me all the way to my Aunt Jackie's house which was in the same neighborhood as Trina's house.

"Hey Con--...Girl, what happened to you?" Aunt Jackie said as she answered the door. I couldn't say anything. I was shaking. I felt cold, and I felt empty. I couldn't respond.

"Her period started, Aunt Jackie. We were on the bus, and someone said she had blood on her skirt." Trina blurted out.

"Is that what happened Constance?" I was ashamed, and I was still trying to process what had just happened, so I said yes and went along with the story. I didn't want to relive it by talking about it, and I was feeling so sick on my stomach. My aunt gave me a change of clothes and took Trina and me home.

When I got home, I went immediately to clean myself up because I was so embarrassed. I don't even remember when my aunt left or if she talked with my parents. I felt like it was my fault that I put myself in that situation because I should not have gone inside, and I couldn't tell my parents or anybody what had just happened. God stepped in at that point and allowed that experience to be blocked out of my mind.

I don't remember a lot after that. I never spoke to Trina again. In the back of my mind, she knew the type of person her brother was. This was not the first time Patrick did something like this based on how she responded. Patrick took my precious virginity and innocence, and he also cost me a friendship. I understand now that it wasn't her fault, but at that age, I was confused, hurt, and damaged. I saw her a few years ago, and she couldn't even look me in the eyes. I told her it was ok, and I apologized for just ending our friendship without having a conversation. We knew what happened. We just couldn't talk about it.

I never spoke about this incident again

until I saw Patrick at my 30-year class reunion in 2018. He was dating a girl that I went to school with. As soon as he came into the room, it was like everything rushed back to my memory. I could see the incident all over again down to what Patrick was wearing that day. I could smell the air in the room change, and I felt that same sickness. I told myself, *No ma'am. We will not give him that much power. Take it back.* I made eye contact with Patrick, and he immediately dropped his head. I knew Patrick remembered who I was. I didn't confront him. I didn't say anything to him. I locked eyes with him. My glance said everything I couldn't without speaking a single word. I wanted him to know, and I wanted her to know what he did to me. I wanted to ruin his life like he had tried to destroy mine. I wanted him to know you didn't kill me. I survived, and you have no more power over me. I had to be in the same room, attend the same events with the person that took my innocence the entire weekend.

I was angry, and I wanted to let her know who Patrick was. I wanted everybody in the room to know who he was and what he did to me. Then, I realized. He's not that important. He wasn't worth my time, my energy, and I am NOT what he did to me. He looked so uncomfortable that weekend, and I made sure of it.

Then, I heard a voice tell me: *Vengeance is mine. You don't know what kind of suffering he's been through, what happened to him, what he lost.*

*So?* I told the voice. To be honest with you, I didn't care what kind of suffering he went through.

*Forgive Him.* The voice repeated.

*Why?* I asked the voice. *He doesn't deserve forgiveness.*

*Uh...neither did you, but I forgave you anyway.* Wow. That hurt. It hit me like a ton of bricks.

*God, help me to forgive him,* I asked. *Please help me to release the pain he caused me. Release me from the protection of the blackout so I can be healed.* I asked. I felt the pain lift, and a peace came over my spirit. I had to let the rape go. Let the stolen moment go. Let the little girl hurt go. So, I let it go.

I started a podcast a few weeks earlier called "Soul Ties" and decided to share my testimony on the podcast. I realized I had to empower myself, tell my truth, my story, and I had to be transparent. I realized that the power of my testimony and the power source to my healing was for me to take ownership of my own story.

After I talked about the rape on the podcast, I had some family members and friends to ask me why I didn't talk about it or come forward so he could be arrested. I told them they were focusing on the wrong part of my testimony. Don't focus on the rape. Focus on the part where God protected me. I survived. I didn't kill him or lose my mind. Focus on how it made me better and not bitter. I didn't want to empower his atmosphere by even speaking his name. Once I talked about it on my podcast, that was the end of it. I didn't want to keep reliving it or rehashing it. I wanted to release it. I thank God that He gave me the strength to be able to do that.

Wherever you are and whatever you're doing: Know that you stole something from me 36 years ago. Today, I reclaim it. Today, I am a fighter, warrior, survivor, and I will not allow another innocent girl to have such a precious jewel that God has given her to be taken away from her again. So, you didn't win. You didn't stop me from living. You didn't end my life. If anything, another life-altering shift began for my life to make me a better person.

Always Remember…

- You never know the potential of the seed that you are carrying.

- One bad decision can change the course of your destiny.

- You are not your mistakes, but you do have control of how your mistakes affect you.

- Find your why. It will change the course of your life and drive your motivation.

God,

I thank you for being a protector of the innocent. I thank you for giving us a tool within our minds and within our spirits that when trauma comes to damage us or kill us, you will provide us with a way to block it out. You will give us a way to suppress it so that we can survive what is happening to us. I thank you most of all that, after the suppression takes place and the trauma has been triggered or revisited, you give us a way in which you can heal us.

Thank you, God, for not allowing us to be stuck. Thank you for allowing us to have an opportunity to get our power back. So many young people have been traumatized and go from being the victim to the predator. God, we ask today that you release them from all of their pain and that this prayer seals their healing.

We pray that the curse will be broken, that it will not be passed on to the next generation, and that they will not lose their voice because of what happened to them. Instead, let us use what the enemy tried to kill us with or what that person attempted to take from us to empower us, strengthen us, and encourage us. Encourage us to go out, share our story, and to become our brother and our sister's keeper. Help us to become responsible and accountable for someone outside of ourselves.

When the trauma becomes too much, give us a place to find peace and rest through therapy, counseling, mentorship or the Big Sister or Big Brother program. Provide them with leadership through a Pastor, teacher, friend, or send someone their way to guide them out of that place of darkness and allow them to recover what was stolen from them.

Most importantly, give us a forgiving heart, God, so we can forgive ourselves. Help us to forgive the perpetrator so we will no longer be labeled a victim. Lord, allow us to come out of our darkness stronger and healthier. Because of you, God, I survived. The stolen moment has now changed my life for the better and has helped to make me who I am.

God, thank you for allowing this experience to be a small fragment of my history and for letting me see that forgiveness was needed for me to be whole. God, you had a plan that I didn't understand back then, but I know it now. May the shifting you allowed in my life help someone to come out of their pit, come out of their place of depression, and to move forward. We bind depression and suicidal thoughts so that you can find a way to get up and fight again.

Until then, God, fight for us. Stand in the gap for us. Cover us by your blood. We decree and declare healing over every reader. You are no longer broken, and may every stolen moment be restored. We seal this prayer in the name of your Son, Jesus, and by His blood never to be broken. May this prayer and God's word for your life accomplish what it was set out to accomplish.

In Jesus Name,

Amen.

Birth Out of Darkness

## *There Is A Seed In You*

There is a seed in you, and it can't wait to break out finally.

There is a seed in you telling you:
> "You can go from the victim's cry to the victor's shout."

The seed in your spiritual belly is growing, and man it's about to burst.
It will tear down strongholds with a sword in its hand while breaking every generational curse.

The enemy tried to kill your seed by poisoning your mind with lies and weeds of deceit,

But your seed has declared I'm stronger now, and I demand my life and my peace:
> Peace in my mind.
> Peace for my family.
> Peace in all of my surroundings.

I'm taking back all that I've allowed to be stolen from me.

I serve notice on every demon assigned to me: The tides have turned, and now It's my turn to do some pounding.

Know the potential of the seed that you're carrying and the seeds that God has planted in your house.
Because of God, I've shifted into my birthing position.
In the words of Diana Ross's song,
    "Baby, I'm coming out!"

In this season, it has not always been easy because God had to toil the land

By getting rid of all the debris, the hurt, and the pain so your seed can produce the best fruit of the spirit it can.

There is a seed in you.
How do you grow it and fertilize it is totally up to you.
With God on your side and if you follow God's plan,
    there's nothing your seed can't do.

# Chapter 3
## *There's a Seed In You*

God is very strategic in his plan. When the enemy is playing checkers, God is playing chess. What do I mean by that? The plan of God always supersedes the plot of the enemy for your life. For every movement in our life, every decision we make, every action that takes place because of the choices we make, God has a plan. That plan is that all things work together for our good.

At the end of Chapter Two, I talked about how rape impacted my life. I didn't want to see another boy or be in any type of relationship because of my first so-called 'intimate encounter'. I wanted to move on with my life after being raped. Now let's fast forward about a year later. I'm learning how to deal with relationships. I had boys that were interested in me but nothing serious. I didn't see the big deal of having a boyfriend because of the expectations of having sex. Based on my experience with sex, that was not happening. I hated the idea of being touched by anyone because of my trauma.

Then, in walks DeShawn Parker. He was only a friend. I was 16 years old and consistently living up to "Ms. Strawberry Shortcake" reputation even as a junior in high school. I played softball along with basketball, participated in theatre when I wanted a different personality, and I still maintained honor roll grades. I didn't really need a boyfriend, but I will admit that I gave him a chance. Our relationship continued, and it got to a point where both of us wanted...well... more. Thanks to my "gift of black out" when it comes to trauma, Deshawn was my first real sexual experience. And then...I get pregnant. Ms. Shortcake. Miss Perfect. Miss Do No Wrong is pregnant. How do I explain this to my parents? Go to school? Play sports? I can't do any of this with a swollen belly. Plus, you did NOT see a lot of pregnant girls at my school. If anyone popped up pregnant, they ended up going to a home for pregnant girls. That "Pregnant at 16" stuff you see on MTV? Not happening in this neck of the woods.

As I carried this huge weight, literally and figuratively, I knew I would have to tell my parents soon. Thanks to my brother, I didn't have to wait for long. We were all in my parents' room one day discussing an event we had to go to, and my brother decides to be Sherlock Holmes.

"Mama! I know why Connie is moody!" He exclaimed. Then, he lifted my shirt. "She's pregnant!" I froze. *What was she going to do? Beat me? Kill me? Send me to a foster home?* These questions ran in high speed through my mind.

"I know." She answered calmly. All of our mouths dropped in shock. I knew I was getting bigger, but I didn't think I was that obvious.

"Really?" I asked quietly.

"Yes. That's why we are going to the doctor tomorrow. Just to be sure before I tell yo' daddy." She answered.

We went to the doctor the next day as promised. He confirmed what we already knew: In six months, I would introduce a new life to this world. The drive home from the doctor was long and quiet. I felt ashamed, and I still had to tell my father when he got home from work.

When my dad got home from work, he sat down with my mother and I to discuss the doctor appointment.

"Hmmm. Ok." He said calmly.

"Daddy, I'm really sorry. I really am." I said trying to break the silence. All he did was nod his head.

"I hope you know your life is over." My mother explained.

"Over?" I asked.

"Yes. You're not going to school. You're getting a job. No more socializing with your friends. Your entire life is pretty much wrapped up in taking care of that baby."

"No school? But mom--"

"Oh no you do not! We are not taking care of that baby. Your child. Your responsibility." She interrupted.

"But how am I supposed to get a job? Without school? Look...I...I know what I did was wrong. If I could, I swear I wouldn't do it! But I need school! Please! At least let me do that!" I begged with tears in my eyes.

"Ok." My dad finally said.

"Ok?" Mom asked.

"Yes. Ok. I know what she did was wrong. I'm not condoning it. But an education is important. So, yes, we will let you finish school.

But you are responsible for caring for the child and its well-being. We will help. NOT raise. Do you understand?"

"Yes sir!" I said, wiping the tears from my eyes.

My dad was understanding but firm. My mother, on the other hand, was determined to make sure I would never forget my decision. My mom made our clothes, and she would get hand me downs from a lady she worked for at the mall. My mother would find the ugliest fabrics and create my maternity clothes. I would have to go to school and even ride the bus with these atrocious garments on my body. One time, she made this big floral dress that I had to wear when my ankles were swollen. It was so embarrassing, and the kids made fun of me for it.

Being pregnant in my household was not fun, but I had one bright star in my gloomy sky: Pamela Spivey. She was a young black African American female. She wore the flyest clothes, high heels, and was one of the most intelligent African American women I knew. I went to her class one day after being ridiculed by my peers during my pregnancy. If I'm honest, I felt like Miss Sophia from *The Color Purple:* "I was feeling mighty low." I was beginning to feel like my mom was right: my life was over. My teacher asked me to stay after class to try to get some extra credit because we were approaching the holiday. It was close to the time for me to have the baby, and she wanted to make sure that I had all of my work for when I went on maternity leave.

"So," Ms. Spivey started, "Have you started thinking about college?"

"Not really." I answered.

"Well why?" She asked.

"According to my mom: 'My life is over.' No college. No future. Just a job and taking care of my baby."

"Your life is over? Girl, your life is just beginning!"

"How am I going to start my life when I have to take care of a new life? Girls like me don't get a chance to do better."

"Yes, you do. If you want it. And Connie... I know you want it. I know you want more for that bundle of joy you are carrying. You do not have to be a statistic, on welfare, and collecting a check. If you want better, work for it. Prove your momma and every naysayer wrong by being a great mom AND being a great woman." I sat and let Ms. Spivey's words saturate my skin. I couldn't believe someone else believed in me. Believed in the future me. Believed in my future seed. I decided that day to be another type of statistic. A statistic of success.

Always Remember…

- God will provide you with a village that supports and wants to see you succeed.

- Mistakes are stepping stones to greatness.

Lord,

I pray for teenage mothers, single parents, grandparents who are raising their grand children. I also pray for parents who are doing the best they can to raise their own kids.

I pray for compassion, understanding and support for when they make poor choices. Teach us how to forgive our mistakes and teach us how to learn from them.

Lord, let us love our children enough that, when they fall short, we will catch them long enough to get them balanced.

God, allow us to trust the plan that you have for their lives and that we will continue to cover them.

In Jesus Name,

Amen

## *Thank You, Son*

My son taught me a valuable lesson.

He said,

*"Mom, why did you allow one person's opinion to bother you?*
 *It is just one voice.*

*You may not have control over what people may call you,*
 *but the way you respond is your choice.*

*It's like you tell me when people don't know the glory behind your story. They think they have a right to chime in.*

*They don't know your testimony, your beginning, your middle or your end. This is your story, and the narrative is still yours."*

You are dealing with people who have also been broken, battered, and torn.

 Provide a teaching moment and God's light to shine.

 Let them know that they don't have to continue to live in bondage.

Show them freedom in their body, spirit, and mind.

My baldness is one of my superpowers; it's not my kryptonite.

The enemy attempts to knock me down, but he better use all of his weapons and all of his might.

Alopecia thought it would rob me of my self-esteem, my hair, my pride, and my dignity. What it didn't realize, however, is that God allowed me to lose my hair after he healed me of all my insecurities. I have all power over alopecia. It does not have any influence over me. God has granted me grace, favor, mercy, and complete victory.

So, no, you don't deserve a clap-back.
There is no need to waste my air.
You're just one voice, with no sound, with your own burdens to bear.

So, thank you, Son, for reminding me to let the life that I live speak for me.

In the words of the singer William Murphy,

"God open my eyes, help me believe, I am what you see."

# Chapter 4

## *I Am Not My Decision*

DeShawn and I didn't have any type of relationship. My parents ended up talking to The Parkers about what DeShawn was going to do since I was pregnant. For the longest time, he denied that he was my child's father, but I knew what type of girl that I was. I know what type of relationships I had. Whether he liked it or not, my son was 50% his responsibility.

Our parents decided to have a chat about responsibilities. Needless to say it was a...uh... interesting conversation.

"That is not my son's child." DeShawn's mom explained.

"Really?!" I responded.

"Ok everyone. Let's back up for a second," My dad intervened. "First, let's deal with the fact that we have two children who are about to be responsible for another person. Mrs. Parker: I know my daughter. You don't have to believe her, but the child belongs to your son.

Second, how are WE going to work together to make sure the child has what is needed?"

Complete silence followed my father's question. After a couple of minutes, I decided to explain my plans.

"Look. With all due respect, I'm going to college. I'm going to be somebody my child can look up too with or without Deshawn's help. I do not want to marry DeShawn. As a matter of fact, we do not even have to deal with each other. But I will do what I need to make sure my son can be the best he can be." After a couple of seconds to digest my words, his parents agreed to help. DeShawn was still in a state of shock, but I can understand why now. We were both children. It was a lot to process. Nonetheless, one of us had to be the mature one, and I didn't have time to wait for him to decide if he wanted to be mature or just a kid.

December 18, 1986. My purpose and my goals in life changed forever. Brandon Mitchell was born. He was healthy. He was strong. He was gorgeous. I prayed that day that I was in the hospital, and I immediately gave Brandon back to God. I prayed that God would help me to raise this child in HIS image so that my son can represent Him in every aspect of life. That is the prayer that I pray every single day for my son who is now 33 years old. Everything that I've ever done, everything that I dreamed of, and every goal that I set out to accomplish, Brandon was the driving force behind it.

I became a single mother at the age of 16. DeShawn moved on with his life and got into other relationships. I never talked badly or negatively about DeShawn to Brandon, even when DeShawn didn't do his part. I didn't want to be one of those mothers that would turn the child against the father. After all, the child had nothing to do with what happened with DeShawn and me. I made sure, however, to let DeShawn know that he will eventually have to have the conversation with Brandon about why he was not accountable.

When I made the decision that I wanted to go to college, Brandon was two years old. This required me to have another sit-down meeting with my parents. My mom's response was the same: "No, you're not going to college. I told you life was over, and your life is focused on your son." I begged, and I pleaded with her. I didn't care about assistance. I didn't care about scraping by. I just wanted the chance to show my son that whatever you want is possible if you are willing to work for it. Eventually, my dad was the voice of reason: "You make sure assistance is in place for 'Scooter' (My Dad's nickname for my son), and we will let you go."

So the journey began. I had to decide what college was going to have the honor of me at their school. My dream school was Austin State University courtesy of my Aunt Tonya. She took us there for homecoming one year. It was amazing. I told myself that I was going to that school. Jessica, my older sister, and Tiffany, my best friend, decided they would also go to Austin State. Keep in mind, we are a family of eight children and two parents. That's 10 people. There was no way that my parents could pay our way through college. So, we knew we had to come up with some type of financial aid for us to get in school.

We both applied to Austin State University, and Jessica got accepted. I didn't get a response back. So, when she went down for her freshman orientation, I went with her. I went with the intention of getting into the school. We went to orientation, and it was the best thing that ever happened to me. It opened my eyes up to bigger opportunities, and it let me know that I had a chance to go to HBCU where there were kids just like me.

Since Jessica was accepted, I decided to tag along with her when she moved in on campus for school. I intended on staying with her until the school accepted me, but God had other plans. After she was settled, we both went to the Financial Aid Office which was in the same building as Admissions. I talked to one of the workers about my situation. Turns out that I was actually accepted into school! My letter was just lost in the mail. It was official: I was on my way to accomplishing my dream. My sister and I were the first two in our family to go to college. We also received financial aid and worked to get through school.

After I graduated, I kept my promise: I told my parents I was ready to take care of my son. My parents kept Scooter until I found a job and apartment. Scooter was finally able to move in with me around the age of 10, and we made the best of it. Was the journey always easy? Not at all. It was a struggle, but I was determined that I would not be a statistic. Scooter and I did not depend on the government or anybody to tell me how to raise my child. We went through a lot together. We survived a lot together, Scooter was my 'ride or die'. He made me realize the results of all the late night cramming sessions, overtime at my jobs, and arduous hours of studying was worth something. And I did it. With a baby and a village of support.

So to every young lady out there that finds

themselves in that same position of being a teenage mom: I wanted to let you know that your life is not over. You will not be a statistic. You will not be a 'welfare mom'. You will not have to depend on the government or anybody to take care of you and your children. You have to use your kids as your driving force, and you have to determine what type of life you want you and your kids to live.

Am I saying there's something wrong with being on welfare? No, because the purpose of being on welfare is to help you get yourself in a position where you can do better. However, I pray that you find the strength to overcome your decisions to be an adult at a young age. I pray that you have support in your village because you have to have people that will help you to get on your feet until you can stand on your own. I pray that you will not allow any and everybody to be in the life of your child. You will make it. You can make it. You've already made it.


Always Remember…

- There really is beauty in the struggle.

Birth Out of Darkness

- Your village encourages you. IF they can not do that, why are they around?

- You are not a statistic. You are not a byproduct of a poor choice but a reflection of how you can benefit from it.

Lord,

You are a God of Grace and Favor.

Thank you for every open door, missed opportunity and for being a God of turning things around.

God, extend your hand to the helpless and give hope to the hopeless. Allow us to know that just because we made a mistake that does not mean that it will control our destiny.

Thank you for making the best out of our disobedience.

In Jesus Name,

Amen

## *Take Back Your Keys*

A man may hold the keys to your prison, but God holds the POWER to your deliverance.

We tend to allow man, which includes ourselves, to have power over our lives and our independence.

The keys represent
>your decisions,
>your feelings,
>your relationships,
>your beliefs,
>your destiny.

You willingly place your life in someone else's hands, hoping they will be able to set you free.

Only God can unlock your doors of bondage and remove you from your misery.

Man can only maintain possession of your keys if you continue to allow it.

So,
>choose to regain your power.

If you created the mess in the first place, just own it.

## Birth Out of Darkness

Take back
>your life,
>your voice,
>your destiny,
>your ability to choose.

God has always held the keys to your deliverance, but he's waiting for you to take possession of them, so you can finally move.

Instead of allowing God to lead or guide us, we recognize the actions and opinions of others to influence us to walk contrary to God's word. This is where imprisonment comes in.

Now we become hurt, confused, stagnant in our process while becoming voiceless no longer having the desire to be heard.

The door that has held you captive, broken, unproductive. Gather your strength and kick that baby in. When you're done, allow God to heal you, so you don't have to walk through that door again.

Who holds your keys?
What are you going to do about it?

# Chapter 5
## *The Promise*

Relationships. I didn't have a lot of them. The ones I did have, however, I got into for all the wrong reasons. I was trying to find myself. I was trying to find value in myself. I was still chasing after the idea that I was an ugly duckling and not the Swan. A lot of my past relationships developed as a result of being the third wheel so-to-speak: I had a friend who was dating someone, and they had a friend. So, we all hung out together. I WAS THE THIRD WHEEL. Now. I said it out loud. I was the ugly duckling that nobody wanted. I was never chosen or pursued by anyone...at least not for the right reasons anyway.

There was always a motive behind being picked by someone. I wanted to be wanted because, in the back of my mind, I could still hear the words of my aunt saying, "You're gonna have to develop a personality for somebody to like you because you're an ugly duckling". Those words plus my rape experience made me never want to put myself in a position to be compromised, disrespected, or my innocence ripped away from me again.

The first time I would consider myself chosen was the summer of my upcoming freshman year in high school. We lived in what we thought was the country in a small town called Bakersville, NC on Cedarfield Drive. A close friend, Darrica Page) and I at the time used to walk to this recreational center. Lord knows that was an exhausting little hump, but we were young and adventurous then. We would go there because they had a pool, we had absolutely nothing else to do, and, of course, we wanted to see the boys playing basketball. Plus, they would have basketball tournaments going on throughout the summer.

We were hanging out in the gym, and the ball came rolling towards us. We ended up tossing this guy the ball. We laughed as young school girls do. Later on, I saw the guy at the water fountain. We had a small conversation, and he and his friend walked us part of the way home. Darrica was interested in his friend, so we saw them a few more times at the gym. I don't know who asked who, but we ended up exchanging numbers and talked all the time. The friend's name was Jason Cooper. The other person's name was Lance Carter.

When school started, I didn't see Lance as much because we went to two different high schools, and he was a couple of years ahead of me. Summertime was our thing, though. Lance became my best friend; we could talk about everything, and his family was the best. I appreciated the fact that Lance never asked me for anything, not even sex. That just wasn't our thing or at least he made me feel that way.

I know you're wondering... "If the relationship was so beautiful, then what happened?" After the first summer, we hung out together. We never established that we were in an actual relationship. School started back up, and life went on. We talked on the phone, and there was a gap in time where we didn't see each other. Then, my junior year in high school, I got pregnant. I'm not even sure how Lance found out about the pregnancy or if we ever discussed it. I did remember he wasn't angry, disrespectful, or judgmental towards me. The cool thing about it was it didn't change the dynamic of our relationship. He was more involved in my pregnancy and my life than DeShawn. It was to the point that everybody thought it was Lance's child! Boy, they were surprised when they found out it wasn't.

So again, if things were so great, why didn't it work out? The answer: LIFE. Lance graduated from high school and started seeing other people (or at least that's what I thought), and I decided I wanted to go to college. I wanted to have a better life for my son, and I felt like the only way I could accomplish that was to further my education. I went to school, and once again, we never established our relationship nor did we discuss what going off to college would look like for us.

My first chance to come home I heard all kinds of things about what was going on with Lance. I decided "Okay...he's moved on, so let me do the same". I wasn't disappointed when Deshawn and I didn't work out, but I was broken-hearted when it didn't work out for Lance and me. Lance and I were on two different paths: He was living that street life, and I needed to focus on school, Scooter, and living a life without Lance in it. There were other contributing factors, but that's a whole different type of story. When I look back on this experience, I realized I never gave myself a chance to heal. I never recovered from the rape, getting pregnant, and my first real heartbreak. All of this created the recipe for the perfect storm of dysfunctional relationships to come.

After being in school for a few days, I felt like we stepped into a scene from the movie School Daze and an episode of "A Different

World". College was everything I imagined it to be, especially at a Historically Black College or University. The experience was amazing! The band was playing, the football team was practicing, Sororities and Fraternities pledging lines on campus, and first-year students walking around looking like fresh meat for the upper-classmen. Amidst all of this wonderful chaos, I remember standing outside of my dorm with one of my homegirls when I see this young man walking across "The Yard" with a burgundy book bag on his shoulders. I heard a still quiet voice tell me; *He is going to be your husband.*

At first, I ignored the voice because I was still trying to repair my heart. I just got here, and I couldn't even see his face from where I was standing. Then, I heard the voice again: *He's going to be your husband.* I told myself *I don't know that boy from a can of paint. How is he going to be my husband* At this point, I was laughing like Sarah when the angel told her she was going to conceive a child in her old age. I told my homegirl Tiffany, "Hey, you see that guy walking way over there with the burgundy book bag? God told me he was going to be my husband." We looked at each other and burst out laughing. I may have been laughing on the outside, but on the inside, I was curious to see who this boy was.

Let's fast forward just a little bit. I got my class schedule, and my first class was History. When I got to my class, guess who walks in? The boy with the bookbag. His face looked familiar, so I waved for him to sit by me. He rolled his eyes like a man. I saw him in class a few times after that, but we didn't talk much outside of dealing with class assignments.

One day when we were in class, this young lady took his class ring and wouldn't give it back to him. Back in my B.C. days (Before Christ) as I like to call them, I was a pistol. Not only did I learn how to develop a personality, but I also learned how to develop a temperament. I had a mouth like a sailor and an attitude to back it up. So after hearing him go back and forth with her about giving back his class ring, I decided to play Little Ms. Intervention. "Look, give him back his ring. Otherwise, you have two choices: Give it to him on your own, or I can take it from you and give it back to him." I demanded. She took the obvious choice and gave it to him.

Bookbag Boy and I eventually became study buddies. I learned his name was Marshal Bishop. Remember, I was used to boys picking me for all the wrong reasons. Studying became something else, and I found myself in a compromising situation where Marshal wanted to do more than just study. Feeling the pressure of trying to make yet another adult decision as a child, I gave in to the temptation. Afterward, I decided to tell him about what God spoke to me about him. This was one of many mistakes I made entering into this relationship. It was after this conversation that Marshal did everything he could to avoid being with me, and he ran as fast as he could in the opposite direction.

On the other hand, I did the complete opposite. I refused to allow me giving up my body for sex to result in me not being in a committed relationship. I let Marshal know that he was not going to be intimate with me, then think he could just leave me. Here I was: broken, insecure, and forcing someone to be in a committed relationship. I forced my relationship on Marshal knowing he wasn't ready, and neither was I. We went through a lot during our relationship in college, but we managed to stay together.

It wasn't until years later that I realized how scary that conversation must have been. Here we were: 18 years old, our first time away from home, in a world full of strangers, we're not in a relationship, and now you telling me

God said we're going to be married. Yeah right. This was the beginning of my brokenness for a purpose. God was preparing me for what was yet to come. The flags were there, but I chose to ignore them because the promise became more important than the Promise Giver. I allowed my promise to kick me out of my purpose. When you put your schedule before God's Plan for your life, then God will take the very thing you placed above him, and He will take you through it. However, you have to be broken.

Brokenness does not mean punishment. For something to change, it has to be broken first. I remembered praying even in college asking God what have I done to deserve all of this heartache and pain. All I ever wanted was to be loved, accepted, and to be chosen by someone. For once, I wanted someone to pick me, to fight for me, and to love me. Then, God reminded me I had someone to pick me, fight for me, and love me since the day I was created. It was HIM all this time, and it will be HIM when no one else will. When they walk out on me, cheat on me, mistreat me, He will never leave me nor forsake me. Since I had no clue of who I was or what I would become, I poured the foundation that defined my relationships. I lowered my standards, I put the promise of a husband before God, and I put up with so many unnecessary things for the sake of saying somebody loves me. When, in fact, I didn't love myself. I didn't know how because I was broken. I was broken for a reason, a season, and a purpose.

Always Remember…

- The promise may not always come in the package we desire but it will come in the package God intended.

- Seek God on when to release what was given to you. Timing and obedience is everything.

- When the promise turns into a nightmare. Wake up, shake yourself off and then refocus on what God told you to do in the first place.

God,

    I pray that we discover that you created us to be more than enough.

    God, although Your word declares that it is not good for man to be alone, it was not Your intention for us to lower the standards and expectations that You have set for us.

    God, help us to surrender our will and our agenda.

    God, we know that the promise should never be worshipped and placed above You.

    God, teach us to follow Your plan and if we deviate from it, help us to get back on one accord.

In Jesus Name,

Amen

Bertrille Williams

## *Baby, Just Breathe*

Let's just take a moment to appreciate this thing called BREATH.

Inhale and exhale.

When all of this is over, know that with God, it is well.

Have you ever been struck so hard in life that you feel like you can't catch your wind?
Have you ever fallen so far in a pit of darkness that you thought you'd never find a way to get back up again?
Have you ever felt alone, lost, or abandoned with no peace within?

When they left you in a place called left,
    thinking it was all your fault and
    left you wondering what went wrong,
It was God's saving grace, mercy, and love that lifted you back up where you belong.

Baby, just breathe. It has nothing to do with you.
Have faith and believe that God has you in the palm of his hand.

No devil in hell can pluck you out, not even

you or any man.
> Endure like a good soldier,
> Be courageous in all that you do
> Advocate for those who cannot defend

themselves.

Romans 15:1: We that are strong ought to bear the infirmities of the weak.
Teach your children to be kind to one another, loving, wise, and meek.
Humility is the key to our blessings, and your character is your foundation.
Always keep God as the head of your life, seek him for revelation.
Be a light in times of darkness and a source of inspiration.

Breathing is a gift from God given to us every day.
There is power every time we inhale and exhale; what we are saying is Yahweh.
Baby, just breathe; it's important, everything about it, including your pause.
This was the very thing that God blew into the nostrils of man; this is how he created us all.
Don't give up on your passion, your dreams, or

your ministry.

Your destiny will happen,
> but in the meantime,
>> baby, just breathe.

## Chapter 6
### B.G. (Before Grace)

When your promise turns into a nightmare, what do you do? Pray. Ask God to wake you up. Why? Because this has got to be a bad dream. I wanted to wake up. Unfortunately, my dreams and reality mirrored each other.

Before I continue, it is really important for me to talk about Domestic Violence. Domestic Violence cases continue to grow in numbers due to the attachment of guilt, shame, and control. The saying "Rule of Thumb" was a law that allowed a man to beat his wife and his livestock so long as the rod used was no thicker than his thumb. In other words, the wife was considered his property just as much as his livestock. By law, he was allowed to beat her. Back then, the wife was not seen as an equal partner: She had no rights, she had no say, and she became an object. As a grown woman who has already been raised and disciplined by her parents, her husband now takes on the role of the father! Mind-blowing, right? Many men and women are currently living out this cycle of abuse and control throughout their relationships even as you read my testimony. There are flags you can recognize and resources out there to get you the help you need. The first step, however, is acknowledge acknowledging to yourself that you are in an abusive relationship.

Let's travel back to my sophomore year in college. I saw a real red flag. I thought we were in a committed relationship. I missed my cycle, and I thought I might be pregnant. When I mentioned it to Marshal, he had the typical response when you're young: "Is it mine? We're not ready for a baby. Are you planning on keeping it?" I let him know that I planned to keep him or her because I didn't believe in abortions.

A massive argument ensued, and he pushed me in my stomach. I fell to the floor, and he stood on my stomach with both feet. "Get off of me! I may be pregnant!" I cried and screamed for him to get off of my stomach. When Marshal realized what he did, he apologized and asked if I was ok. He told me he was drinking with some of his friends, and he didn't know what came over him. I saw for the first time what his temper could do. "I'm sorry. I'm so sorry! It's the alcohol. I promise."

He kept apologizing, saying it would never happen again, and it was the alcohol. I accepted his apology and warned him that it better not happen again.

Later that night, I started bleeding. I had no clue why. Either way, we never talked about that incident again. I didn't set boundaries or a standard for myself when it first happened. To be honest, I didn't know I could.

Three years later, I graduated from college, moved back home, started working, and raising Scooter. Our long-distance relationship wasn't working out for us, so someone had to relocate. I felt like I had sacrificed enough in our relationship: I didn't want to raise a child in the city, and I didn't want to move away from my family. So I told him that, if he wanted us to work, he would have to relocate. We initially decided to live separately because Marshal's Dad was planning on retiring and moving back to North Carolina. So, Marshal would stay in his Dad's house in NC and find a job. In a few years, we would consider moving in together. Notice I didn't say get married but live together. Marshal thought marriage would be 'hard'. (SIDE NOTE: Bam! There it is, ladies! A man will tell you upfront what he wants and what you should expect, but we have selective hearing. This is what I heard: "We will live together first, and then we will get married.")

I'm an old-fashioned country girl, so Marshal had to get my Father's blessings. I was raised in the church; my Dad was a Pastor, and my Mom was a minister, so "shackin' up" (living together) as they called it in the South was not an option. We both agreed that, out of respect for my parents, we would talk to them about our decision to live together first with the plan to get married.

My parents got home around 11 PM from a revival the night we decided to talk to them. My mom went straight to her room and closed the door. My dad took us in the living room to talk.

"I wanted to honor your daughter by asking your permission for her hand in marriage. We plan on living together first. Then, we will get married later." Marshal explained.

"Hmm. Ok. Scooter, how do you feel about this?" My dad asked.

"I like him. I'm really happy to finally get a dad." Scooter answered. My dad stayed silent for a couple minutes. He kept looking at

Marshal, Scooter, and me.

"Marshal," My dad started, "I appreciate you taking the time out to wait for me and have this conversation, but I don't believe in shacking or living together before marriage. She's a grown woman. This is her decision to make, so I can't tell her what to do. I can only tell you how I feel about what you all are planning on doing. This is my daughter and my grandson, and there's nothing I won't do for them. I'm a Dad, and I love my children. As long as she's happy, I'm happy." I exhaled for the first time.

"Thank you, Mr. B--" Marshal started.

"But," My dad continued, "I'mma say this to your face...man to man. Nigga, I know you got a mean streak in you. I see what God is showing me. Before you put your hands on her, you better bring her home. Because if you don't and I hear about it, Nigga I'm gone look for you, and I'm going to put you in a body bag. Do you understand?"

Marshal straightened up. "Yes...Yes sir." Marshal answered. I sat there looking puzzled. What did my daddy see that I didn't? He never put his hands on me. Well, since that time Sophomore year. But that was because he was drunk. Otherwise, we were ok. My dad, however, saw something spiritually that I refused to see naturally.

"Ok. You can have her hand, but I meant what I said. Before you put your hands on her, bring Constance home." My Dad said sternly. I was so excited that my Dad had permitted him to marry me that I didn't take heed to my dad's warning.

Always Remember…

- God will always give us a glimpse of what to expect when we don't take heed to His warning signs.

- What you never want in a relationship is to be molded or shaped by the decision you made to place a person in the position of God in your life.

- When dysfunction shows up in your relationship and life don't wait to deal with it later, face it head on.

- Don't allow guilt, shame, or the opinion of others to keep you in bondage or a toxic relationship.

God,

Thank you for not allowing what was intended to hurt me to kill me. Help me to separate myself emotionally from matters that should be walked in spiritually.

God, grant me the wisdom to understand the promises of God do not supersede the plan of God.

Lord, help me to not allow my heart and my desire to be loved to cause me to lower the standards you have set for me. Sharpen my discernment to know when a relationship is God ordained and not enemy sent.

In Jesus Name,

Amen

Bertrille Williams

## *Your Grace*

*Your grace and mercy has brought me through.
I'm living this moment because of you.*

I love the lyrics to this song.

It reminds me that God loves me despite all of my wrong.

If it wasn't for God's Grace and mercy, I acknowledge I would have lost my mind.

But God placed a hedge of protection around me and said that *You are mine*.

Never take His grace and mercy for granted or feel you have a sense of entitlement.

Because Jesus paid the price for you and took on all your punishment.

So, God, I'm forever grateful for all that You've done for me.

Without You in my life, I would have no love, no joy, and no peace.

# Chapter 7
## *Five Years of Grace*

Eighteen months later, we got our first apartment together. All that was left was the marriage. Every girl dreams about the perfect marriage proposal. This is the time that you have dreamed about all your life. You imagine your Prince Charming coming to sweep you off your feet or your Knight in Shining Armor rescuing you from the world and everything in it. Yeah...I didn't get a fairy tale wedding proposal at all.

We had probably been living together for about three months, and I decided to give my life to the Lord. I decided that I didn't want to live together unless we were married. We had a huge blowout, and Marshal stormed out of the house. When he returned, he threw a ring box on the bed and said: "Here. I hope you're satisfied." He stopped by the pawnshop to get his bracelet fixed and he saw a car with the words "Just Married" painted on it. He took it as the sign he needed to get the ring. "Now don't ask me no more about getting married." Marshal shot back. I sat there in shock. I never even received the question! This was my fairy tale storybook proposal.

All my anxieties that I had dealt with for years, insecurities that I would never be picked or loved, and reminders that I will never be the one for somebody came flooding back to me. I pushed my disappointment to the side and became ecstatic about getting an engagement ring. I know you're saying to yourself. 'Girl, What in the world was wrong with you?' My response: I was broken. I got the wedding ring in September and planned a wedding six months later.

Everything that could have gone wrong in planning this wedding went wrong. The tuxedos didn't come in on time. The group that was scheduled to sing was a no show. We barely got the bridesmaid dresses done in time. The photographer messed up the pictures. The limousine was late. I was sick as a dog the day of my wedding. God was loading me down with flags. But, you know me: I got this God, and I don't need you to intervene. Remember... this is the promise.

A few months after getting married, my husband lost his best friend. I'm a firm believer that we wrestle not against flesh/blood, and spirits can be transferred from one person to another. Marshal's friend was very abusive to his wife physically, mentally, and emotionally. They fell out behind Marshal's friend hitting his wife. The day Marshal's friend passed, Marshal said he felt his friend's spirit pass through him. I also found out during this time that my husband had grown up with domestic violence in the home. (Domestic violence is a gradual process. The victim is slowly torn down verbally, emotionally, mentally, and financially way before physical abuse is introduced. Isolation from family and friends taking away your support system while making you feel like they want to have you all to themselves. The core value behind it is control.) During this time, Marshal and I had been together for over ten years, and the power was already gone.

Because the methods were so subtle, I realized what was going on too late. I was going through the stages of abuse before the physical was introduced. It began with grabs, pushes, restraining you, holding you down, covering your mouth so no one could hear you. It escalated to punching, choking (strangelations), threatening to kill you and your family. The worst time I remembered was not being able to read the Bible in the house. I had to read it outside. I walked through the house like I was sleeping with the enemy to make sure everything was in order. Marshal would wake me up in the middle of the night to clean tires in the wintertime. He belittled me in front of one of his friends, choked me until I could barely swallow, and even put a gun to my head. I always got a sick feeling whenever he was around. It was like my spider senses would let me know about good and bad nights.

I had company over when I wasn't supposed to have anyone in the house. Marshal would vacuum the rugs a certain way so he could tell if someone came over. I attempted to clean the same way, so he didn't know someone came to visit. When Marshal came home late from a second shift, he woke me up.

"Connie...Connie! Who's been in my house?" Marshal asked as he violently shook me.

"What?" I asked.

"I said...who was in my house?!"

"Nobody!" I lied. He yanked me out of bed to show me footprints that I forgot to vacuum up.

"What I tell you about having people over here? I don't like people in my house Connie. They don't need to know what's going on here! Keep people out of this house..." Usually, he continued this long lecture which was exhausting because that was worse than the physical abuse.

"Ugh! Get over it Marshal. It's not a big deal." I thought I told him in my head. Well, instead of saying it in my head, it came out loud.

"Excuse me? After all I do to provide for you and your son, you got the nerve to tell me to get over it? Do I complain when I'm working two or three shifts? Do I have people over? No! Cause I don't have time because I'm feeding your lazy behind and your son! You know what? I'm sick of this." He headed over to the closet. I was looking down trying to ignore him when I felt something cold and metal press against my head. I froze. I slowly moved my head to look up at Marshal. His eyes had a rage I never saw before.

"Bitch you gone die tonight! I'm tired of you always disrespecting me!" He shouted. I prayed Scooter was in his room sleeping.

Normally, I would have him go to a friend's house when I knew Marshal was in a mood.

"I work hard to provide for this house! I'm sick of you always disrespecting me! Bitch you gone die tonight!" I saw a flash of red run across his eyes. Then, I heard a still voice say *sit down, shut up, and don't move*. I prayed and pleaded for the blood of Jesus. My prayers must have reached Him because I felt the gun move away from my face. Marshal backed up and looked at his hands. Then, he collapsed on the floor and pleaded with me "Help me. Connie, I'm so sorry. I...I didn't know I was...I'm sorry. Please pray for me." I got on the floor and prayed for him because, at that moment, I realized demons were real.

The abuse went on for the first five years of our marriage. I was the typical victim. I left several times, didn't tell anybody about it, covered up my bruises, and tried to keep all of it away from Scooter. I wrestled with the thought of killing him or killing myself. I became empty, afraid, and stuck. The next day I was driving down the highway with my hands off the steering wheel begging God to take my life, but I didn't want anyone else to get hurt while he was doing it. My car ended up coasting into a church parking lot, and I was listening to this preacher. It's like God was speaking directly to me. The man of God said "I don't know who you are sitting in a church parking lot, but God wanted me to tell you it's not your time because you have work to do. Lay your hand on the radio so I can pray for you." He prayed as if my life depended on it, and it did. He told me to call into the radio station because he needed to hear that I was okay. My God saved my life that day, and He's been saving it every day since.

I tried my best to shield Scooter from everything, but I couldn't. He came to me one day and said, "Mom, I'm about to fuck him up! I'm tired of Marshal putting his hands on you!" I knew I had to do something. Scooter and Marshal had gotten into it before I got home from work over something, but God said *Get out now. If you don't, somebody is going to end up dead*. Based on the way they were looking at each other, I didn't want to be responsible for something happening to either of them. I asked Marshal to allow me to get some clothes. He could have everything in the house. Scooter and I just needed to leave. I told my son to pack some clothes and wait for me in the car. I got us in this mess, and I would get us out of it.

When people tell you they will help you if you ever need anything, be prepared for them not keeping their word. We left that night with nothing but a basket of clothes. I went to my first option I thought I had and explained everything that happened. Her response: "Ok. You can stay tonight, but where are you going to stay tomorrow?" Wow! She told me several times I could stay with her because she was alone. She had a three-bedroom house with no kids or husband. I was mad at first, but God reminded me that He was my source. If needed, He would provide all my needs. I thanked her and told my son we were leaving. I drove around, apologizing to him over and over, trying to figure something out. I had no money, a half tank of gas, and I had to go to work in the morning.

I called my best friend Brandy Jones next. I hated to call her because she was my go-to place every time I left, which was numerous times. She was a single mom of three, and I remember her kids would always ask how long we were staying each time. But she never hesitated, judged me, and she always opened up her home to us. When I got there, I told her I had to do something because if not something bad is going to happen. She told me I could stay as long as I needed it. That night I cried and laid before God pleading for Him to take my pain away. When I finally went to sleep, God showed me three people in my dream who were going to sow into my life so I can get out of the situation I was in.

When I woke up, I talked to Brandy about what God had shown me. I got dressed, called out of work, picked up an apartment guide, and started driving. I specifically asked God to send me to my sanctuary. I needed a place where I could find myself again. As I was driving, I got a call from a friend of mine who lives in Virginia, and she sowed $100 into my life.

"I'm not sure what you're going through, but God told me to tell you it's already worked out." She explained. I thanked her and hung up. When I hung up the phone, God reminded me of the dream. She was one of the people God had shown me! As I was driving, I heard a voice that directed me to an apartment complex. As I drove up, the manager was leaving for lunch. I asked her if I could please take a look at an apartment. She stated that she was usually gone for lunch by now, but she came back to get her purse. I explained my situation, and she showed me her model apartment.

"You came just in time. We are running a special this month!" The manager explained. When I walked into the apartment, there was light everywhere. I heard the angels singing. My first response was, "Wow! I could live here!" She took all of my information and told me what I needed to move in. Remember, I have no money, and it would be 30 days before my next check. I had nothing but a basket of clothes, a half tank of gas, a car note, and two people to take care of. God reminded me that He would supply all of my needs. I went back to Brandy's house excited because I found a place. I didn't know how I was going to pay for anything, but I felt a sense of peace come over me. Brandy said, "Look. I wasn't sure about how serious you were with leaving. I understand it's a process. So when you left, I began praying for you. God laid it on my heart to give you $100 because you were going to need it to move." We both cried. Of all the people who knew my journey, it was her.

Once again, God reminded me of the dream I had. At this point, God is blowing my mind at how quickly He was moving! A co-worker called and asked where I was. She and her husband decided to fill up my gas tank and gave me a kitchen set for my new apartment. I was bawling at this point. My phone rang again. It was the manager at the apartment. She explained that I qualified for certain discounts because of my job. So instead of it costing me $350 and first-month rent, I only paid $200 with first-month's rent being waived. God was amazing. Everything was falling into place. I went back to my husband's house, grabbed my clothes and Scooter's bedroom set, and closed the door on that chapter of my life….for now.

I moved into the new apartment with what we had. The second we moved in, I laid on the floor and made angel wings on the carpet. I praised God like I lost my mind. There was no way I should have been there. My co-worker came by and delivered my kitchen set. She said somebody left a box of food and cleaning supplies on my porch. It wasn't a small box of food either. We started setting up the table to eat, and my phone rang. Another friend donated a brand-new Queen size bedroom set because she knew I didn't have anything to sleep on. My sister Jessica called me and told me to pick out a living room set, and she would pay for it. Blessings were coming from every side.

The first twelve months of living there were nothing but a miracle. We had prayer service, praise, and worship in that place so much that my friends called it "The Upper Room". I struggled at times to pay the bills, but I always had food and necessities. During that time, I kept a journal about how I got to this point and how I became this fragile, scared woman. At the end of the lease, I renewed it for another six months because I planned to get a divorce, move to Atlanta and start my life over.

I asked God to monitor my contact with my husband and to deal with his heart, so when I asked for my divorce there wouldn't be a problem. God honored my prayers. The few times I interacted with him, we got along better. I was close to the end of the 18 months, excited about beginning my new life, so I asked God for a "sure 'Nuff sign" (That's exactly how I said it) that this marriage was over. (SIDE NOTE: Be careful what you ask God for because it may not come in the package you want.) Our relationship and interactions were amicable, but I still wanted to move on.

To celebrate our good space. I allowed Marshal to come over for dinner. We watched a movie, and he decided he wanted to be intimate. Against my better judgment, I allowed it. A few weeks later, I got sick on my stomach.

"Are you pregnant?" My best friend asked with a giggle.

"I got a 17-year-old graduating from high

school and I'm about to get a divorce. What do I look like being pregnant?" I answered.

"Well...only one way to find out. You know the Dollar Store sells them? Go ahead. Pee on that stick girl!" She answered. We came back to the apartment with all three tests. The pee didn't even hit the stick good when the positive sign appeared. I didn't believe it, so I went and got a blood test. Pregnant!

Always Remember...

- Grace is given to us not because we deserve it but because God loves us.
- The hand of man may have hurt you but Hand of God will heal and save us.

Lord,

Not my will but your will be done. Teach me how to apply this principle to my life. Help me to understand that what I want may not equate to what I need. I pray for the gift of forgiveness for each of you so that you can move forward with your life.

In Jesus Name,

Amen

Birth Out of Darkness

# *I'll Just Adjust My Crown*

When you try to knock my Crown off my head,
Pulling out my jewels of purpose,
Derailing my destiny with the words that you said.

I'll just adjust my crown.

When you try to distract me
      by throwing my Crown to the ground,
I'll just pick it up, dust it off, and continue to make myself proud.

Excuse me while I adjust my Crown.

I came into this world kicking and screaming while covered in someone else's blood.
I have no problem going out the same way.

Keep that in mind when you set out to try and ruin my day.
The people who wanted to bury you didn't know you were a seed.

They didn't expect you to rebound, let alone succeed.

They didn't think you'd heal from all the hurt

they caused

They didn't think the dirt they threw on you was exactly what you needed.

You survived what you thought would break you.

Now straighten up your Crown, move forward, and tell your pity party
    That's enough. We're done.

What didn't kill me, better get on its mark and get set, because now it's your turn to run!!!

# Chapter 8
## *Change of Plans*

Jeremiah 29:11: "For I know the plans I have for you, declares the Lord. Plans to prosper you and not harm you, plans to give you hope in the future."

*Wow! God, after all these years and just when I was about to get my life back on track, you choose pregnancy to be my sign. I finally had my confidence, strength, peace, and joy again. Now a baby! So are you just going to make me start completely over?*

God reminded me of a conversation I had with Him years ago after I had my first child. I specifically said, "God, please forgive me for hurting my parents and disappointing them. I've learned from the mistakes I've made, and I'm thankful for the gift you gave me, my firstborn son. But God... if you ever decide to bless me with another child, all I ask is that you let me be married next time because I don't want to have another child out of wedlock and please allow me to have the baby before I turn

35." God honored my prayers, and I made sure it never happened again. So I had the sign that the marriage wasn't over.

Having a child 17 years apart was not the answer I was looking for. (Side Note: Word to the wise: Be careful how you pray and what you ask God to show you because you might not like the answer He gives you.) Everything I asked God to do during our 18 months of separation, He did. Going back was not a part of my plan.

"Mom, do whatever you want to do, but I'm not going back to that house. I don't care how much he's changed. I can't do it." Scooter asked if he could stay with his friend until the semester was over, and then he'd finish out his senior year with his grandparents. This forced me to make one of the worst decisions of my life. I allowed my son to stay with one of his friends. I cried until I couldn't cry anymore. I was angry because I felt like I was choosing to make my marriage work over the happiness of my son. He was 17 years old, and neither one of us should have been forced to make that kind of decision. However, the plan was for him to finish the semester and then live with his grandparents until graduation. I thought it was the best decision for Scooter because he had so much anger inside of him based upon the things I had exposed him to. I should have fought harder for Scooter, put us first, or put my foot down. Because I was pregnant and all of my plans were blown out of the water, I decided to give my marriage another chance.

When I first told my husband about the baby, he was shocked. His first response was like we were two high school kids. I felt like I was 16 years old again, sitting in my parent's living room, and trying to decide what was our plan of action. After the shock wore off and it was established he was the father, we decided to make this marriage work. Everything was great at first. He was involved in the pregnancy process, went to all the doctor's appointments, and even started communicating better. Once the baby was born, I actually believed we could do this thing called marriage.

My oldest son kept his word and moved in with his grandparents. I rarely got a chance to see or talk to him because Scooter felt like we were replacing him with our new baby, which was furthest from the truth. Just when I felt like my life was coming together, it was falling apart. I was dealing with a newborn son alone because my husband is working all the time. My oldest child hates me and lives with his grandparents, and I'm trying to mend a broken marriage. I'm exhausted, my stitches are about to burst from the C-Section, and I find myself sliding into depression. It was so bad my doctor warned my husband to get help for me before I died from complications. We started to get somewhat on a routine schedule. I went back to work, and we found a phenomenal babysitter.

Then, I started to notice some changes in my husband's patterns. He started coming home later than normal, and his scent had changed. Some nights he would smell like fresh soap. Some nights he would come home and go straight to the shower. My spirit and my woman's intuition said he was having an affair, but my heart didn't want to believe it. He had some nerve! First, you put me through five years of abuse. I lost my son behind your tail. I almost bust my stitches open taking care of your son, and this is how you thank me? With an affair?! When I asked if he had something to tell me and that it would be best just to come clean, he would deny it. Everything in me told me I was right. It was just a matter of time before God would reveal it to me. One day, I got tired of feeling like I was crazy, so I started praying. I fasted and prayed for about three days. I asked God to reveal it to me. (SIDE NOTE: Never tell God what you're not going to go through. Man, how did I keep missing that lesson?)

The next day my husband woke up with his face partially paralyzed. He couldn't blink, and he was only able to talk out of one side of his mouth. The doctor diagnosed him with Bell's Palsy. It caused the muscles in your face to become temporarily paralyzed. There was no medication to take to correct it or surgery needed. He was told it was something that would correct itself over time.

"Marshal...you're doing something you don't have any busy doing, and I asked God to show me. Come clean. Are you doing something you shouldn't be?" I asked.

"I don't know what you're talking about." He responded from the right side of his mouth.

"Okay." I answered.

A week later, he swallowed the gold cap he had on his tooth in his sleep. I looked at him like Celie when Mister tried to cook for Shug on *The Color Purple*.

"Do you need to tell me something?" I asked.

"No." He answered.

"Okay." I answered.

I told my Dad I felt like he was having an affair, and I asked God to show me. He asked me if I was ready to receive it. I honestly couldn't answer that question at the time. He prayed with me, and I didn't think anything else about it. I decided to throw myself into my work and taking care of our son, Justice. I didn't care what he was doing because I knew eventually God would show me.

A few months passed. I was at work and received a call from my husband.

"Somebody wants to talk to you." He said. He handed the phone to the person.

"Okay?" I answered.

"Hi," She started, "My name is Veronica Bankston. I...I've been having an affair with Marshal for the past three years."

"Excuse me?" I asked.

"I've been seeing Marshal for the past three of years."Those words kept reverberating in my ears. Three years. THREE. YEARS. I started backtracking and realized...he was doing this while we were...trying to...make this marriage work!

"Wait a minute!" I screamed.

"Constance look--" Marshal started.

"Wait. A. Minute. We're not doing this. Right now." I hung up the phone. Someone ripped my heart out of my chest, showed it to me, and asked what am I going to do about it as they walked away.

I told my co-workers to take me home. I opened my front door, collapsed on my living room floor, and screamed "Why? How could you do this to me?" My friends were scared and thought something happened to my Dad. I couldn't get my words together, let alone wrap my head around what I had just heard. Marshal destroyed twelve years of marriage on a three-way call! I didn't even get a face to face conversation. Wow! I did what I knew best, so I started praying. I cried, I begged, and I asked God what I did to deserve so much pain in my life. God told me, *GET UP! GET OFF THAT FLOOR! The very thing you bow down to becomes your god, so get up!*


Always Remember...

- Let your SHOUT (praise) be greater than what's shouting on the inside of you! In other words, whatever is your inward struggle, inward voice or whispers of doubt about who you are....let them be silenced by the voice of God, the victory cry and the calling that's upon your life. So go beyond the victim's cry to the VICTOR's shout!!!

God,

Empowers my voice. When I was silent, I became a victim. Magnify my sound so I may speak against the things that come to harm my temple and attack my home. My home is my heart, my family and my salvation. Most of all, heal me.

In Jesus Name,

Amen

Bertrille Williams

## *Victim's Cry to Victor's Shout*

When life knocks you down: Get up!

When you find yourself all alone and you're trying to scream but can't manage to make a sound: Cry out!

Life is full of twists and turns.

Filled with heartbreak and lessons to learn.

So what if they misused, abused, and mistreated you?

It's not what was done to you that gave them power, it's what you didn't do.

You didn't fight back. You accepted what was said and took the posture of a victim.

Take what happened to you. Make weapons of warfare to win your victory.

You are a warrior, a curse breaker, and an overcomer.

You have victory. You will not walk in the spirit of a victim any longer.

Live your best life without an apology.

Take back everything the enemy stole from you and declare:

I have the victory!

# Chapter 9

## *Get Up!*

*Say God...you not even going to avenge me or comfort me? You're just going to yell at me and tell me to get up. Where is the fairness in all this?*

God reminded me vengeance is His. It was clear and obvious that I wasn't going to win this argument. So, I gathered my thoughts and kept saying to myself, *Get Up*. I couldn't see anything because my eyes were swollen just about shut from all the crying I did. After I got up, I straightened up my clothes, and I kept saying to myself, *You're going to be okay*. I told my friends I'm going to be fine, and it was ok for them to leave.

After they left, I called my Dad. I told him everything that happened, and that I wanted to kill my husband just like he killed me. My Dad reminded me of the conversation we had just a few weeks earlier.

"Well...you did ask God to reveal." He

answered.

"Yeah, I did--"

"And...I asked you if you were prepared for the truth."

"I know but--"

"And you said you didn't know if you were prepared. How can you be mad at God for something you asked for?" My Dad was right. I did ask for this.

"Ok. Ok. You were right. But how? How do I deal with this...pain? I just wanna...I wanna cut his tires, bust out his car windows, and make him feel every bit of the pain that he has caused me!"

"Listen and listen well. I know that you're hurting. I know you want to get even, but you're a child of the Highest God. First, you are my seed, and you're better than that. Don't you ever let the actions of a man take you out of the presence of God and make you act out of character. God will deal with both of them, but what you have to do now is show him Jesus. At least he told you. That should count for something. You have to decide if you're going to forgive him or leave. I support you either way."

"Wait...what? Give him Jesus?! I don't want to give Marshal to Jesus! I want him to pay for everything he's ever done to me!"

"Look, you can say you want him to pay, and you can convince yourself that it's right to feel that way. But in the end, you can be right. But... are you, God right? The answer: No, you are not. When the time comes, you will do exactly what God tells you to do because you belong to Him, and because that's how we raised you. God is going to birth something out of you through all of this. You may not see it now, but God will get the glory out of your pain." We prayed, and I hung up. Then, I cried until I had no more tears left.

*Who do you think I am, God?* I asked. *I have sacrificed so much of myself for this man, but I keep getting his tail to kiss. How is this fair? How do they get to kill me, and there's nothing I can do about it?*

*Because I will birth ministry out of this.* HE answered. *Jeremiah 29:11. For I know the plans I have for you declares the Lord, plans to prosper you and not harm you, plans to give you hope in the future.*

I tried to get to some normalcy. I got up to get some tissue to wipe my eyes, and my house phone rang.

"Hello?"

"Hello? Who is this?"

"Is this Constance?"

"Oh...I'm sorry. I didn't mean to call you. I was looking for Marshal." She answered.

"No. You called the right number. HE wanted you to speak with me."

"He who?"

"God."

"Ok?" She said confused.

"Let me introduce myself. If you would have known who I was and whose I was, you would have never gotten involved with my husband. I'm a child of the Highest God first, and I'm about to minister to you." When I tell you God had me minister to this woman, I ministered like she was on life support, honey. God revealed everything she had ever dealt with in her life. God went back to her childhood trauma and explained to me that this was her second time getting involved with a married man. She was the woman at the well. God was allowing her to thirst after Him and to break her cycle of being someone's side piece.

We talked for almost two hours, and God had me pray for her. She apologized. She said she would have never gotten involved with my husband if she knew I was a woman of God. I laughed! I explained that this would have happened regardless. I also told her I didn't solely blame her because she only did what he allowed her to do. I informed her that one day she was going to find her happily ever after. Then, her life would be shattered by a phone call like mine because Karma knows every body's address, and she doesn't forget anybody's name. She thought I was cursing her, but I explained I wasn't. I was simply stating facts.

I couldn't believe that God would put me in the position to minister to the person who just tried to destroy my family and me! If that wasn't enough of a test, my husband walked in the house as soon as I got off the phone and asked me to forgive him and pray for him. Without hesitation, I prayed for him, but forgiveness was way down on the bottom of my list of priorities.

A couple of days after praying for Marshal and his mistress, I called my Dad. He told me that the hardest was yet to come: forgiveness. If I decided to leave, I would have to forgive two people: Marshal and myself. "I know that's hard because it is fresh," He started, "But it's needed. Remember, you've done some bad things yourself, and God still forgives you." Well, he had a point.

In the next few weeks, I wanted him to suffer like I was experiencing just being honest. I grilled him every chance I could. I wanted to remind him of what he did, and if I wasn't at peace, neither would he. At some point, God will not allow you to continue down a path of destruction without warning you. It wasn't long before HE had something to say about it.

*You have to make up your mind what you're going to do. You are going to either forgive him, or you need to leave. You are not allowed to be the judge, jury, and executioner; vengeance is mine saith the Lord. How do you expect me to heal the house if you keep going behind me and tearing it down? You can't do both. I won't allow it.*

I asked God to help me to forgive. (SIDE NOTE: When God wants to use you, He understands that what you're going through has nothing to do with you. God is concerned about your willingness to be obedient despite what kind of mess you're in.) I told God that if He got me out of this pit of darkness, I would never let another woman go through alone.

God got me out of the hole. Not only did

he do that, but He also gave me several ministries out of my pain. I shared my story at several women's conferences about abuse, adultery, rape, suicide, depression, and marriage. I started the *Unspoken Word Women's Ministry* where, in over ten years, countless women had a place where they could be vulnerable and safe while giving God their broken pieces so He could make them whole. I also had a blog for over two years based on the ministry. I also started *Guardians of Grace*, a mentoring program for young ladies transitioning into womanhood.

    I had a talk show with a dear friend of mine that you can still find on Facebook and YouTube. I talked with local high schools and colleges about domestic violence. I currently supervise a unit that deals with only domestic violence cases. I also do a podcast called "Sole Ties" and now my first book. Look at how God can change your plans. The Plan of God always supersedes the plot of the enemy. Everything you are dealing with, no matter how hard it may be, God has a plan.

Always Remember…

- Give God all of your broken pieces, so he can make you whole again.

- God always warns us before the storm comes. It's up to you if you allow Him to shelter you from the rain.

- From the victim's cry to the victor's shout, I am not what you did to me. I am a product of what I decided to do with it.

God,

    Bless and heal the broken hearted.

    God, grant them peace in the midst of their storm.

    God, I decree that joy, love and life be restored.

    God, repair relationships, minds and spirits. Teach us to forgive, to minister to our enemies and to take our tragedies and turn them into victories.

    In Jesus' Name,

    Amen

## *Utilize Your Gifts*

Proverbs 18:16.

"A man's gift makes room for him and brings him before great men." Your gifts are a testament that we are overcomers, and trials will eventually come to an end.

It doesn't matter if you sing, mime,
do magic or speak a word over this world.
Your gift was a tool God blessed you with
to be an inspiration to our little boys and girls.

So, when you sing, do it unto the Lord.

When you speak words, use your authority.

Put your list aside and make God's plan for your life a priority.

Comic Steve Brown: Thank you for allowing God to use you to bless us
with this quarantine talent show platform.

You gave us a chance to share our talents,
our gifts while forming lifelong friendships and bonds.

So, ignore all of the negative remarks and

continue to be brave.
You never know whose life you may touch or who's life your gift may save.

Stay focused and remember why You started this QTS in the first place: To spread love and laughter while providing us a judgment-free safe space.

Continue to use your gifts to spread joy
and never allow your character to bend.

Remember Proverbs 18:16:
"A man's gift makes room for him and brings him before great men."

## Chapter 10

### *Birthing of a Ministry*

I always knew that God had something special for me to do. Did I ever think it would be a ministry? NO. It was the complete opposite. I thought it would involve singing or comedy. I have a bucket list as everyone should. Preaching the gospel was nowhere on that list. As I look back over the shifting moments that made me who I am, the ministry was always the result.

I gave my life to the Lord in September of 1997. I remember sitting in a night club one night a few months before surrendering my life to God and looking at the people. You know how the fluorescent lighting would show all the lint on your clothes and faces? I saw glimpses of the spirits people were carrying. I'll admit that was a little scary. I remember hearing a voice say *Get up. It's time for you to leave*. I shook it off. I just paid my money, and it was still early! Then the voice was louder: *It's time for you to leave*. Then out of the corner of my eye, I saw this guy pull out a gun. I told my girlfriend to get down. I heard what sounded like a popping sound, and I heard something whiz by my ear: gunshots. My girlfriend and I crawled our way towards the exit.

We made it outside, and people were running towards their cars. Once we got in the car, we checked each other to make sure we were okay. I told her "Girl, if we make it home tonight, I'm going to church tomorrow and giving my life to the Lord." We laughed about it on the way home, but I knew I needed to make some changes. The next day my Mom got us up with the usual "Rise and shine. Ain't nobody sleeping around here. Get up and get dressed because we're going to church." Church was not optional in the Bishop household.

I can't even remember what the sermon was about. I just remember feeling like I was being yanked out of my seat, and I found myself standing at the altar with my hands up with tears streaming down my face. On that day, I surrendered everything to God, and my journey to ministry began. Every dark moment in my life, every tragic event, and every choice I made after that point directed me towards the ministry. After I gave my life to the Lord, I was sold out. I wanted to make sure I was living a righteous life. I firmly believe that if I hadn't surrendered my life when I did, the outcome of my journey would have been different. I think I would have lost my life, taken a life, lost my mind, or been incarcerated if I didn't find a way to the altar.

On my road to ministry, I experienced a lot of breakthrough moments. Moments that helped me to realize that God has a plan for my life. I never really connected the dots until now. I got married February 14, 1998. July of 1998 was when my husband's best friend transitioned from this life. We purchased a brand-new home in July 1999, and the five years of abuse started a couple of months after that.

During that time, I was juggling a lot. I was trying to see where I fit in the church, discovering what my purpose/gifts were, dealing with the chaos brewing in my house, and learning a new position at work. I had left my Dad's church and joined one of my brother's ministries in Raleigh, NC. As a part of the new member's class, we had to complete the book <u>A Purpose Driven Life</u>. That's when I discovered that the plans God had for my life were greater than the expectations I had for myself. I had been married close to three years at this time, and the church was my way to escape from the abuse that was going on at home.

I got a phone call from my sister in law requesting me to be a speaker at a women's conference in Beaufort, South Carolina. The conference was entitled "Resurrection Power: If you don't know my story, then you can't understand my praise." My topic would be "Refused, Abused, and Misused." Mind you, I've never done anything like preaching, speaking engagements, let alone a whole conference. I was scared. But deep down in my spirit, I knew this was from God, so I talked to my brother about it. My brother told me I wasn't a minister. We had a few words over it, so I decided to tell my Dad like we were kids. My Dad asked me if I prayed about it, and he asked what God told me to do. Neither my brother nor Dad knew what was going on with me and the domestic violence because I was trying to handle everything on my own. I told my dad I felt like God had called me to share my testimony during this conference.

I like to say that the conference in South Carolina was the day my "water broke" in ministry. God performed miracles and surgery on me that weekend. The way God used me during that conference was amazing. This was the first time that I was able to discuss my abuse without crying. I felt empowered. The enemy, however, was waiting for me when I returned home. The abuse was escalating. I asked God if I was doing something wrong. I had just had this phenomenal time only to return to the same mess. God responded simply: *I have need of thee.*

A few days later, I got a call from my supervisor on my job asking me if I would be interested in doing a position that would require me to deal with domestic violence cases. Clearly, God has a sense of humor! *Well...think about it,* God started. *Who better to do this than someone who is currently walking through it? You can see it from both sides.* I told my supervisor about my situation, and she said the same thing God had just spoken in my spirit. She told me if I needed anything she would be there for me. She also let me know that it would be kept between us unless I said otherwise. This meant so much to me, so I decided to focus on my new job and to make a difference in someone else's life. (SIDE NOTE: Don't you know when God has a plan, it's always bigger than you?)

I was the first domestic violence officer, and I also talked with local schools/colleges about domestic violence awareness. In May of

2003, I accepted the call to ministry. My initial sermon was called "From Pain to Power!" I was in about my fourth year of abuse, but I got stronger and stronger every time I entered the pulpit. I became an Elder in the church a couple of years later. I was Sunday School Superintendent, Women's Ministry Lead and Praise/Worship leader. My spiritual life was on point, but I was still struggling in my personal life and my marriage.

When the affair happened, I had to preach a sermon the very next day called "How Bad Do You Want It?" *God,* I started, *who do you think I am? I'm not built for all this pain. How am I going to preach about the affair. It's still fresh!* God said, *Preach your way out of the pain.* That sermon reminded me of when my water first broke in ministry. There was such a powerful move of God that day. My path in ministry was filled with extraordinary moments. I have witnessed powerful movements of God, but all of that was a birthing contraction for the ministry that was to come. The true birthing of my ministry didn't happen in a church or pulpit at all. The day God's true ministry for my life happened was August 11, 2008. That was the day my Bishop, Pastor, Mentor, Counselor, Best Friend, and my Dad died.

There's an old saying: "Death comes in

threes". After 50 years of walking this earth, I am certain this is true. On August 11, 2008, we lost Bernie Mac, Issac Hayes, and Ruben Mitchell, my dad. I heard it on the news that we lost two awesome entertainers, and I warned my husband that somebody else was going to die because "Death comes in threes". Then my phone rang. It was my Mom. "It's your daddy. He's been taken to the hospital." I hung up the phone, called my girlfriend Brandy, and asked her to ride with me to Bakersville.

When we got to the hospital, my uncle was standing in the parking lot. When I saw his face, I knew my Dad was gone. My uncle hugged me and took me to see my Dad. It was the longest hallway I ever walked, and it felt like we were walking in slow motion. When I came around the corner, I saw the Highway Patrol (My oldest brother was a trooper), a chaplain, the doctor, nurses, and a few others I can't remember. When I entered the room, he looked asleep. My niece was holding his hand singing, and my Mom was rubbing his forehead. My mom asked me to pray to God to bring him back. As I prayed, God warned me. *I'll do it, but keep in mind the quality of life he'll have.* I looked at him. He looked at peace like he was smiling. He was still warm, but I knew he was gone. At that moment, I knew it would be selfish of me to ask him to return to all the chaos in the world. I couldn't do it. I kissed him and told my mom I would call everyone else.

I called each of my siblings, and I noticed a man in the waiting room crying. He told me he worked with my dad. He was with him when it happened. He said they were in the paint store laughing when he felt my dad hit his shoulder. Then, he was on the floor. Doctors said he was gone before he hit the floor, and he didn't experience any pain. My Dad always said if he died that he wanted to go out laughing or praising God, so he was able to go out on his terms. He was only 60 years old, which was entirely too young. After that, things happened so fast.

The morning he died he called me like he usually did. We talked every day before I went to work, during the day, and after work. He was excited about a dream he had. He told me that he was at this huge church. Two men took him through a side entrance and up a tall ladder on the side of the building. When the men got to a certain point, they told him this was as far as they could go and told him to keep climbing until he saw an open window. When he got to the window, a man was waiting for him, and he looked like a tailor. He measured him and told him to put on this white robe trimmed in gold. It looked like the robe the Pope would wear including a hat with a staff.

"Man... is this all for me?" My Dad asked.

"Yes." The man responded.

He then led him to this stage and allowed him to look out over the crowd of people waiting.

"Who are these people waiting for?" My dad asked.

"You. These are all the lives you have touched." The man answered.

He said he woke up crying, and God told him to come outside. He went out and stood on the porch. God told my dad that, just like Abraham, your seed would be blessed, their children would be blessed, and God showed him everything he was going to do for his family. My Dad told God that if he were to die today, he would be okay because he knew his family would be okay. I talked to my Dad at 7:00 AM that morning. He passed around 9:00 am. My Dad's homegoing service was exactly what God had shown him. So many people came to pay their respects for him. To this day, if I run into anyone who knew my Dad, they would say how he changed and impact their lives. He had the biggest smile, gave the best hugs, would do anything for anyone, and he had a Shepherd's heart for God's people. He was a soul winner.

When my Dad died, I felt lost. I went through a David and Saul experience in ministry. I had to run for my life. I didn't know where I fit in anymore, and I slipped into a period of depression. I didn't feel like Ibelonged anymore. I started Pastoring out of hurt and pain. I was trying to recapture what was lost at least, so I thought.

I was doing ministry at work, and now my body is starting to give me warning signs. My depression was getting worse. I started pulling my hair out due to the stress of ministry, marriage, and life in general. I had nobody to talk to because my Dad was my person. So I had water everywhere, I was bleeding out, but the ministry was being birthed. At this point, I was birthing spiritual babies, but I didn't have the energy or drive to continue to take care of them all once they came. Then one day, as I was lying in the darkness just ready to give up and die, God spoke to me. *I alone am God. There is no other God before me or above me, not even your Dad. Your father's ministry had nothing to do with a church building. His ministry was about winning souls. His ministry still lives within you. Let go of the church and everything attached to it. You want to carry on his legacy? Pick up your mantle and do what I called you to do. Win souls.*

I got up, and I told the people at my church that I was closing the doors because I needed God to work on me. I prayed and asked God to deal with me. I no longer wanted to preach out of a place of hurt. I didn't want to lead people broken. I didn't want to continue fighting a losing battle, and I needed to release myself of the guilt of not praying for my Dad to stay.

God began a work in me immediately after that. I birthed several in-person and social media ministries, but I learned that I couldn't do it all. I'm not in control, and I have to take care of the ministry God has given me. Since then, I've released some other things. My motto is "Do thy duty that is best and leave unto the Lord the rest." When I got to this point in my life, the darkness began to lift, and my life has been shifting ever since. I've grown a lot, and I'm still on the potter's wheel. So now I'm standing in the SON light, adjusting my eyes, and singing "I can see clearly now the rain is gone, I can see all the obstacles in my way..."

Always Remember…

- What was intended to kill me God used to heal me.

- If you never get the acknowledgement or the apology you feel you deserve are you willing to forgive them anyway. Don't allow your pain to keep you in a place of hurt.

- God can restore any relationship if you allow Him to restore you first.

- Ministry is not what's in the four walls but what's in the walls of your heart and soul.

- Don't depend so much on a person regardless of who they are that when they die you die with them. Your loved ones expect you to pick up the mantle and continue the work

God,

Bring comfort to all that are grieving the loss of a loved one.

Bring them comfort and bring them to a place of acceptance. To accept the perfect Will of God and that death does not mean the end of life.

God, through your strength we will heal, endure and overcome the pain that comes with death. Most of all let us find peace in knowing that to be absent from the body is to be present with the Lord.

In Jesus' Name,

Amen

Bertrille Williams

## *Missing You*

Since the day you went on to be with the lord,
    I had a void in my soul.

I didn't want to move on without you and parts of my heart waxed cold.

Then, God stepped in and reminded me that death Is not permanent and Jesus took back the keys.

Death has no victory and God took back death's sting.

I miss you.

I find joy in knowing that you're ok.

When this life is over,
    we will be united again some day.

# Chapter 11

## *A Place of Hurt and Pain*

Before my Dad passed, I had a rocky relationship with my Mom. I knew my mother loved me. I didn't necessarily believe she liked me. My Dad and I had a close relationship because I was truly a Daddy's girl. We talked every day especially when it came to ministry. I'm not sure if my mom felt left out or she just wanted to share the same relationship with my Dad. My Mom and I were fairly close. When I rejoined my Dad's ministry, things became distant. Prior to my Dad passing, I held several positions in ministry: Elder, Minister, Praise/Worship Leader, Sunday School Women's Ministry Leader, Superintendent, and Prayer Leader. I know that's a lot for one person, but we had a small congregation.

My Mom called a meeting the same day of my Dad's wake to let me know she was stripping me of all my positions in the church, and that she was the new pastor. I remember seeing the anger in her eyes towards me. Instead of expressing how I really felt, I shared with her that I understood she was coming from a place of hurt. I ended the meeting before we said something we both would regret. "Before I let you have this church, I'll run it into the ground!" She responded. I'm glad I know who I am in God because that conversation would have taken me away from ministry. This was my Mom. I'd just lost my Bishop, Dad, and best friend. Then, I realized: My Mom had also lost her husband, Bishop, and best friend.

I sat in the pews crying the following weeks. The church was hurting. My mom was hurting. I was running for my life from my own Mom. I asked to leave several times because I felt like the church was suffering, but I was denied a chance to leave. I finally got the okay to leave, but my mom and I didn't talk as much or see each other that often because I was hurt. When I tried to talk to her about what happened, my mom denied anything ever happened. No acknowledgement or apology.

The turning point for me was when I asked God to help me to love her in the place that she was even if she never acknowledged what happened or never said she was sorry. She was still my mother and the only living parent I had left. God did exactly what I asked for. He helped me to realize my father's legacy and ministry. Who he was as a Pastor was never tied up with a building. He was a soul winner, and God had given me a Shepherd's heart just like my daddy. So, I forgave my mother because she was operating out of hurt.

It took some time to release the pain because the hurt ran deep. When you allow God to heal your pain and bring you back from a place of brokenness, however, healing becomes easy. I never thought my Mom saw me. I still felt like that little girl who wanted her to tell me how proud she was of me and how much she loved me.

So I committed to doing the work. I started calling my mom more, visiting more, and letting her in on what I was accomplishing in my life. We are a lot closer now. She's constantly praising me and telling me how proud she is of me. I'm proud of her as well. To be married to the love of your life for almost 40 years and lose him while feeling distant from your children is a lot for anyone. I was able to share with my Mom that she played a major part in me becoming who I am, and I thanked her. I know that meant the world to her. I'm grateful for where we are now in our relationship. She supports everything I put my heart and mind to do. I can truly say she's one of my number one fans.

Always Remember…

- Remember that hurt people hurt people, but they tend to hurt people worse.
- All broken relationships can be mended when you allow God to do the healing.
- God is a repairer of the breach.

God,

Thank you for mending broken relationships.

Thank you for allowing time and your word to breath life back into what appears to be a dead situation.

God reminds us that although pain comes with death, there is also life in the memories that have been left behind.

Thank you for allowing us to recognize that a person's actions are tied to our emotions and to charge it to their heads and not their hearts.

In Jesus' Name,

Amen.

Bertrille Williams

## *Keep Trying*

When life seems to be falling apart all around you,
> keep trying.

When you're told no, you're not good enough, or you'll never amount to anything,
> keep fighting.

When dream killers, dreams stealers come, and they will, in an attempt to take out your vision, which consists of your eyes.

When they try to tear down your self-esteem, get in your way, get inside of your head by filling your ears with deceit and lies.

Deny them access to your hopes, your visions, your dreams.

Let them know I am an earth-shaker, a curse breaker, and I can accomplish anything if only I just believe.

How bad do you want it?

Do you want it more than you want to breathe?

What are you willing to give up or sacrifice to succeed?

# Birth Out of Darkness

Keep trying.

Keep fighting.

Keep believing.

Before you know it, there's nothing you can achieve.

You're standing on the backs of your ancestors who worked hard by the sweat of their brows.

It's in your bloodline to slay the Giants that get in your way.

Whatever you do, never give up and, by all means, never stop trying.

# Chapter 12

## *Here Comes The Flood*

When a person is drowning, you expect a lifeguard or first responder to come along and save them. They are both trained to administer CPR or render some type of first aid. When you are drowning in life, where are the first responders and who renders your first aid spiritually? I found myself in the position of drowning after my Father passed, and I decided to release the ministry after 4 ½ years of pastoring. I was struggling with depression. I was fed up with ministry. I felt depleted physically and spiritually. I just wanted to be left alone. I was drowning, but no one heard my cries for help. No lifeguard. No first responders. Nothing.

I thought about all the women I had ministered to over ten years, all the sheep I had been a Shepherd over, all the speaking engagements I was invited to, and all the lives I had encouraged. You mean to tell me I couldn't get anyone to come and check on me?! I found myself struggling to keep up the appearance that everything was alright, but I was secretly suffering. I continued to do ministry, encourage others, and cry myself to sleep at night. I wasn't happy in my marriage, I was beating myself up for a failed relationship with Scooter, and I was becoming numb. Even the strongest of people have moments of weakness. But where does the strong go to find a place of rest? Where do they go to fall apart and who do they trust to allow them to discuss their innermost struggles?

You go to therapy. That's where you go.

I never thought that I would find myself sitting on a couch, listening to waterfall music, and spilling my guts to a man who looked like "Where's Waldo". When I went to my first appointment, I didn't know what to expect. I thought it would be like what you see on television. I would be lying on a couch talking with a therapist with a note pad who would want to put me on some medication.

Instead, I was given the following instructions:

> A. I had to commit to 6 months of therapy.

B. I could come as much as I like, talk about whatever I want, and pray with the counselor after each session.

C. Oh, and I had homework assignments.

*Homework? Are we in therapy or school? Well, it's worth a try. It can't be worse than what I'm dealing with now.*

The first question he asked me was "So...what is God leading you to talk about?"

"Aren't you the therapist? You tell me." I responded.

"Ok. Why are you here?" He asked. It was like the dam broke, and here comes the flood! I finally found a place to lay my head. I spoke my truth without interruptions or the conversation turning into helping someone else with their problems. During my 18 months of therapy, I was able to release some of my childhood trauma, discovered how I ended up in an abusive relationship, discovered my Momma issues, and I was a people pleaser. I also learned I had abandonment issues, I was angry about losing my Dad, and I put way too much pressure on myself. I cried until I couldn't cry anymore, and I put in the work. Once I got past blaming other people, I had to put the mirror up to myself. I had to learn to love myself. I didn't recognize it at first, but I had to deal with my root because everything I had experienced was a symptom of that pain.

At the age of 35, I had to go back and deal with the seven-year-old little girl. I had to learn how to breathe life back into her. I had to become her lifeguard and first responder. This was my conversation with her.

*Look, you had some life-changing words spoken over you, but I'm here to tell you they were all lies. The words were intended to break your spirit, give you a complex/low self-esteem, and derail your purpose. This leads to years of overcompensating for who you are and causes you to make some poor relationship choices. Just know it was not all bad because the words lost power the day God showed you who you are. Overall, don't worry; you took those same words and fought your way back from being thrown into a pit of despair. You crawled and clawed your way out. You became an advocate for all the seven-year-old girls just like you. You can now release her so God can heal your pain.*

I moved on to the teenage girl who lost her innocence to a monster.

*Baby, it wasn't your fault. Yeah, you made some mistakes. Every teen does that. You got pregnant. It happens. But remember: parenthood does not come with an instruction manual. You did the best you could with what you had. You were a good mother. You sacrificed everything for your kids. Forgive yourself. Forgive. YOUR. SELF. Forgive the abuse; you were a victim like Marshal. You are no longer a victim. You are an overcomer! You overcame it ALL. Now, you have your power back. Forgive your mother even if she never says sorry. Enjoy the time you have with her, and remember she too has a story. God called you for HIS own, and your Dad lives in you.*

This was my last therapy session. I remember finally feeling empty, and I haven't been in therapy since. That was about 15 years ago. Do I ever think about going back? Yes. Letting out your pain and having a safe place to be vulnerable is always needed. Instead, I take advantage of talking with God because, like therapy, he doesn't interrupt me, he allows my time to be about me, and he gives me homework on self-improvement. I don't have it all together, but I'm getting there. I made a promise to all of my past selves.

*I promise first to give everything I am and have to God. I will never abandon you. I will allow you to heal. I will put you first, I will practice self-love, and we will never be victimized again. There will be days where we will struggle with God. God will send someone to encourage me. God will present me an opportunity to speak life into someone else while speaking life into myself. God will remind me that I'm more than enough. The floods come to wipe out everything that doesn't belong, it moves things around, and it leaves everything bare. This is a chance to rebuild, to show your survival skills, and to let you know you're stronger than you realize.*

Thank you, God, that the floods came because they were necessary.

Always Remember…

- God has prepared you for the flood but you have to make the decision to get out of the water before you drown.

- Take time to reflect on all your past hurt, trauma, and ask God to reveal the lessons behind the experience.

- Therapy is necessary because everyone needs a safe place to lay their heads.

God,

Open up the floodgates of anointed waters over the lives of each of us.

God, allow the waters to cleanse, purify our hearts, minds and souls.

Give us Godly counsel to assist us through the process of healing.

Allow our transparency with you, through therapy to give us a second chance at life.

Our pasts were never intended to keep us in bondage but to take us to a new level in our relationship with each other and with God.

In Jesus' Name,

Amen

## *Beast Mode!*

*Good morning devil, Yep it's me again.*
*Despite your plots, despite your plans,*
*God decided last night was not going to be my end.*

*Excuse me while I yawn and stretch before my feet hit the floor. Let me gather my thoughts, say my prayers, awake my sleeping giant from within, and tell myself,*

"Get up, let's go and serve notice on the devil I ain't taking your mess no more!"

I'm no longer a victim, nor will I play the role of being weak. I discovered I had the power all along to place my enemies under my feet.

Beast mode is defined as a state of performing something with extreme strength, skill, or determination.

That's precisely what God had in mind when he made you one of his creations.

You were created as a spiritual solution to a global problem that no one else could solve.

You were born a warrior with the ability and skills to conquer it all.

Walk bold, Lion and Lioness. Have some dignity for yourself and lift your head.

Remember, you are what God has Called you and not what people have said.

Make the enemy tremble every time you get out of bed.

Tap into your beast mode and put a bounty on your enemy's head.

## Chapter 13

### *Shift Your Position*

Everything about you and everything tied to you can change in a matter of seconds. When I decided to forgive myself and release my hurting girls, my life changed instantly. I felt a sense of peace, relief, and energized. I became excited about ministry and life again. I had finally dug my way out of a place of darkness, and I had the wounds to prove it. I asked God, what's next? Now God truly has a sense of humor in His response at times. I got my next shift in life in the way of a Praying Mantis and a grasshopper.

I was on my way to a doctor's appointment when I noticed a Praying Mantis on my driver's side mirror. *Look dude. I'm on my way to a doctor's appointment, so you might want to get off now.* I told the Praying Mantis. He made a slight shift in his position. I put my truck in Drive and started down the driveway. *Ok,* I reminded Mr. Mantis, *this is your last chance because once we hit the highway, it's a rap.* The Praying Mantis shifted slightly again. At this point, I'm curious as to how long he will stay on and what it will take to make the Praying Mantis fly off. I get on the interstate. My speed changes from a residential limit of 25 to about 70. I continue to watch the Praying Mantis to see how this is going to work out. He continues to shift his position, expands his wings at certain points, but he never stops shifting. The shifting was small, and there was no panic in his posture. He maintained this position until we reached the doctor's office. Once I parked, the Praying Mantis jumped off. *Wow, he made it.* I thought to myself, but the message didn't hit me yet.

    After I finish my doctor's appointment, I notice a grasshopper on the windshield of my car. I attempted to shoo him off, but he made the decision to stay. I gave him the same speech I gave Mr. Mantis: *If you're going to get off, now is your chance.* I started driving. Instead of staying where he was, the grasshopper decided to jump on the hood of my truck. It didn't look like a good spot because he started slipping. At that point, the grasshopper decided to jump off, but his timing was all wrong. He jumped off just as another car was passing. Yeah...it didn't end well. I laughed a little. *Welp, you should have done like the Praying Mantis and shifted, Mr. Grasshopper.*

*What did you learn from the Mantis and the Grasshopper?* That voice asked. *The Mantis decided to maintain his position. Although it might endanger his life, it's safer to stay where he was. The mantis didn't panic when the speed picked up when the wind blew harder. It just made slight adjustments. Even when it shifted at times, it needed its wings to keep him stable. He understood that even though his life was endangered, it was better than jumping in traffic and losing its life. Once he reached a safe destination, he jumped off because he had made it. The grasshopper on the other didn't trust the position he was in and decided to jump in a less stable place. When that didn't work, he decided to jump, but his timing was off. If he would have waited, he could have got off in a better spot because I was about to stop. Instead, he jumped and was hit by an oncoming car, so his decision cost him his life.*

God reminded me that, like these insects, I'm going to be put into positions that would cost me if I make the wrong decision or take the wrong position. It may cost me my life, my peace, my position in Him. Just because it looks dangerous doesn't mean it is. The Praying Mantis found safety in his dangerous position while the grasshopper allowed it to make him commit suicide. *Look at all the shifting moments in your life and how you adjusted.* The voice answered. *Life came at you fast just like the speed limit changed. The winds of change hit you hard, and it may have caused you to rely on your wings to stabilize yourself through it all. It taught you how to shift. You shifted to survive. You shifted your thoughts, your prayers, your posture, and you learned to trust what God had placed on the inside of you. Like the grasshopper, you put yourself in a precarious position. You attempted suicide, but then you shifted back to me just in time.*

Things can change in a matter of seconds, but like the Praying Mantis, stay in your position until you get to a place of safety. I learned God shifted me back on the road to recovery. I was so excited I had to share this revelation with anyone willing to listen. I called a close friend of mine and told her about it, and I discussed it on my social media outlets and show. God truly blessed us through that season. It felt good to get back into ministry. I still felt like something was missing because I wanted to get back into the Women's Ministry, but I couldn't see myself giving up another ten years of laboring.

I got back into writing on my blog, but it didn't give me the personal interaction I was used to. I was no longer pastoring, doing the talk show, or the blog. I was spending time with myself, and I was comfortable with that. I didn't completely shut the world out. I was still ministering to people then I saw this young man on Facebook talking about "Hugs With Love". He would travel the world giving out hugs. *God, I can do that.* I started the "Hugs With Love" Project, which was a huge success. I initially started with the homeless. If you can't hug the homeless, you can't hug anyone.

The next year I did a project with the elderly, but I didn't get to do the children's project. I'm still learning from the Praying Mantis and the Grasshopper. Life is full of changes, and you won't always see them coming, but you do have a choice as to how you respond to the changes. I like to think that in my 50 years of walking this earth, I've shifted in so many directions. Each shift allows me to grow while shedding pieces of the old me. I've gone from putting everyone first and trying to be the one who gets picked to choosing me as a priority. I'm learning to hear the voice of God as I shift. I'm listening for when to stand my ground and when to jump off and when it's safe to let go. If you ever want things to shift in life, ask God to do the shifting.

I'm amazed at all the things God has protected me from. He's had a constant hand over my life even when I wanted to jump off like the grasshopper. It would be impossible to include every shifting moment that made me the woman that I am. I'm just grateful for each life-changing moment. You have a choice: Will you be the praying mantis or the grasshopper? Either way, you have to decide to shift. Shift your mindset. Shift your posture. Shift your position in life. Most importantly, Shift your relationship with God. The shift can make the difference between life and death for you and everything attached to you. Shift your position, and it will shift your life.

Always Remember…

- When you change your position, it makes it difficult for the enemy to catch you.

- The shift you make can make the difference between life and death for you and everything attached to you. Shift your position, and it will shift your life.

God,

    Give me the posture and spirit of the praying mantis.

    God, when the enemy comes in like a flood, allow me to shift my position. Don't allow my fear of the unknown to cause me to become the grasshopper and jump off prematurely.

    God, shield my eyes and cover my ears so i won't allow what i see and hear to make me commit spiritual suicide.

    God, as you make shifts in my life give me the stability to hold my position, the patience to endure the process, the wisdom to know when to shift and when it's safe to jump off.

In Jesus' Name,

Amen

Bertrille Williams

## *Slay Queen Slay!*

It's not often that you come across a Queen who can slay by not doing anything at all.

Instead, she kills because she's bold, confident, and beautiful.

She doesn't have to walk around with a
    Crown on her head,
        wearing a swimsuit, or
            displaying herself in an evening
           gown.

She slays with a smile on her face, a swag in her walk, an attitude of a warrior, and her skin on her head is her Crown.

You see, she chose to set her own standards;
    to let go of the stereotypes that tell you
        your beauty is defined by the amount of
hair on your head,
    the shape of your body, and by the tone
of your skin.

She is represented by her intelligence, grace, by the mark she leaves on this world and the light that shines from within.

So you go, girl! Girls rule the world!

## Birth Out of Darkness

Queen, you definitely do rock!

Never allow anyone to define you again
    or put you inside of anyone's box.

You are a fierce Queen, so honey set this world on FIYA!!

Walk-in your destiny with every inch of dignity you
    have while declaring to everyone

I've got the ultimate power.

The power to reinvent myself if I want
    to knock down every excuse.

You have the potential to be the best version of you with no apology.
You are no longer a slave to what society defines as beauty,
    because can't nobody slay this thing called Queendom like you.

So to every Queen out there,
    Slay Queen Slay no matter what the cost!

You are fine as wine walking this thing
    called life out like a straight-up BOSS!!

Slay Queen Slay! You are what you answer, too,
    and not the words that they say!

Bertrille Williams

Don't let anybody's words define you but
    the way you choose to live your life
    let that speak for you every day!

Slay Queen Slay!

# Chapter 14

## *Rising of a Phoenix*

A Phoenix represents transformation, death, and rebirth in its fire. As a powerful spiritual totem, the Phoenix is the ultimate symbol of strength and renewal. In this sense, it never truly dies. Instead, it is an immortal creature continually rising from the ashes. It is a symbol of rebirth, life, growth, longevity, and it usually marks a new beginning or event in a person's life. I've always been fascinated by the myth of the Phoenix. Although it's consumed by fire, it still raises from the ashes even better than it went in.

When I came out of my dark place and found the light again, I got a tribal tattoo of a Phoenix because I felt like after all I had gone through, I rose out of the ashes a different person. I have four tattoos: a black panther, (at the time I got it because I thought it was cute, but later I discovered how powerful the panther is), a butterfly with a pink ribbon (for my dear friend who survived cancer more than once), a Daddy's Girl, (for my Dad because no matter how old I get, I will always be that) and the Phoenix. I know some people don't agree with marking the body with tattoos, but they represent my fire moments and how I emerged as a new creature. The Rising of a Phoenix marks where I am in life now. I've gone through the fire, the flood, the darkness, and now God has birthed me out of the night.

My Phoenix season started with losing my hair. I started losing my hair at the age of 25 due to having an allergic reaction to some hair glue. I was also pulling my hair out as a form of nervousness when I went through the domestic violence period of my life. This resulted in having huge bald spots throughout my head. I tried everything, but I continued to lose my hair. I went through a period of wearing wigs, which was pure torture every time I would put the wigs on. I locked my hair and had sister locks for over ten years. Although my hair was down my back, I still had bald spots in my head. I wrestled with cutting it all off for over a year before I made the decision. July 18, 2015, I decided to have an "Embracing My Baldness" party with a few friends at the barbershop and cut it all off.

I have been completely bald for five years now; it was the most liberating thing I have ever done talking about rising from the ashes of societal stereotypes and how beauty is defined. Who the Son sets free is free, indeed. Your freedom is tied to your actions and your beliefs.

The next Phoenix moment gave birth to my "Sole Ties" Podcast. I got a call from a college classmate wanting to interview me about my journey with Alopecia and making the decision to shave my head. I was more than excited to share my testimony about the day God freed me from the bondage of thinking my life evolved around my hair. We did the podcast, and he showed me how simple it was to do a podcast. I decided to give it a try. Sole Ties was created on September 2, 2019.

I created a platform of transparency, motivation, and a place for God to be God in my conversation. I wanted people to take a walk in another's man's shoes and to become appreciative of the shoes they have been given. We often look at the lives of others and think they have it made, but we are getting an outside view. I was interested in creating a Godly difference and not to waste people's time with fruitless conversation. Sole Ties has been such a blessing for me first because God has still decided to utilize little old me even after all the mess I was and the mess I was in.

Following the podcast phoenix, it was time for intricately inspired words and sentences to rise from my experience. How did that happen? From a social media show.

January 2020: Covid-19 (AKA Cornavirus). By March, we faced a crisis that none of us were prepared for. We were also hit with racism and the fight to make Black Lives matter due to the outrage of the killing of innocent black people by law enforcement. We were truly in the midst of so much chaos. The country was racially divided, and the number of COVID deaths was vastly increasing.

In the midst of all this, I came across a comic by the name of Terrance Taylor on Instagram. He was hosting a nightly talent show called "The COVID Talent Night". I watched it a few nights and decided to muster up my nerves to send a request to come to the show. For the Gospel Sunday edition, I decided to sing "I Won't Complain" (which was one of my Dad's favorite songs for me to sing). I was nervous, but I did it.

Since Terrance is a comic, he found some laughing points to my song. The funniest part of the show, outside of Terrance, is the comments. People will give you their honest yet funny critique of your performance. I noticed some of the comments were a little mean and directed at my baldness, which didn't sit well with me. I decided to let my clap back be my come back. In other words, I decided to respond with a clap back poem. I wanted to express myself positively, but I also wanted to establish that I wasn't that girl. So on April 14, 2020, my poetic Phoenix rose out of the ashes.

My first spoken word was entitled, "Don't Come For Me!" After that night, poetry just started pouring out of my spirit, and I became known for my spoken word on the show. I also earned the nickname Motha Fav because my Instagram name was *Favored4this*! That nickname still makes me laugh. During this Quarantine season, we develop a family-like bond. God opened the door for ministry. We shared our struggles, our victories, and we encouraged each other to pursue our dreams. I always felt like God had placed some type of book within me. There was no way I could experience all that I've been through in my life, and not one person benefits from it. I'm a firm believer that our trials and tribulations are not for us but a means of helping someone else.

I put off writing a book because I felt like I had nothing to say, who would benefit from it, and just because it affected me didn't mean it could impact someone else. It was ten years ago that God told me to release my story, but because of my pain, my trauma, and my poor self-image, I didn't do it. It was the Holy Spirit and Terrance's encouraging words that helped me have the confidence to put pen to paper: "I don't know why I keep hearing this, but God said you need to release that book. You are such an inspiration to this show and such an inspiration to me. The world needs this book, and I need this book. If you don't do anything else for me or write another poem, please write that book!" Just like that, a fire was ignited once again.

A few days later, God woke me up out of my sleep and gave me the full vision for the book. I received the title and the cover illustration. God did everything else. He has placed every person in my path to continue to push me towards the goal of finishing this book. It was scary at first because I didn't know where to begin. What would be my shifting points? How am I going to get this published? *Stop asking. Just write.* I listened to God. You are reading the result.

I want you to realize just because it happened to you does not mean it owns you. There is a rising Phoenix in all of us, but you have to let the fire do what it's designed to do.

Birth Out of Darkness

God's refining fire will cause all of your infirmities to rise to the top, so he can purify you. God wants it all. He understands it stands in the way of you being made whole. You have to be willing to release all of your excuses, stop blaming others, and make changes in your life.

Always Remember...

- Don't come out of the fire empty handed.

- Your joy comes from within. Why allow any outside influences to change that? Only you can allow someone to change your mood. Don't let your atmosphere change you change your atmosphere. The power of influence flows through you, not your environment.

- Strength is coming out of your struggle! BELIEVE IT....you are coming out stronger than when you went in!

God,

Thank you for being the author and finisher of our faith.

God, thank you that you never waste a chapter of our life.

God, you know the final outcome and you are in the business of giving us a comma instead of a period.

God, you are always looking to expand our expectations and give us a better version of life than what we think we are reading.

God, thank you for not allowing the fire to consume us but to change us. You can change our outcome, change our destiny, make us the hero and not allow the villain to win in our story.

God, thank you for making my life a best seller and for even considering my life worth telling.

In Jesus Name,

Amen

## The Hands of my Ancestors

When I look at my hands,
I don't just see my struggles.
I see the efforts of my parents, my
grandparents, and so many others.

I can only imagine how those same hands
that worked the farms that belonged to
someone else were the hands that were
used to push and pull their plows.

They are the same hands that
clapped for joy as
they worshipped their God, embraced,
and loved their children.
While paving the way to make it so,
we can enjoy the lifestyles
we have become accustomed to having now.
The hands of my ancestors were tired,
wrinkled, full of callous, and sores.

They displayed scars of their struggles and
marks left behind from fights they had
endured.
There is also beauty, softness,

and strength in those hands.
Hands that were made because of people
trying to break them, but their spirits
refused to be broken by any man.
When I look at the hands of my mother,
they tell me a small part of her story.

How she held the palm of my father for over
40 years of marriage, and then she used those
same hands to say goodbye to him when God
decided to take him home to heaven.

How she used them to help take care of her
eight children while owning her flower shop,
which was one of her life's dreams.

How she used them during her prayer time
to cover us while asking
God to bless her children
to walk as Queens and Kings.

So, when you look at your hands,
you're looking at the hands of your ancestors,
your legacy, your bloodline, your history,
and your inheritance.

Be proud of what you see, be careful what you
allow your hands to touch and who you allow
your hands to embrace.
Remember, their hands are a part of you, and
the hands of God created you for a purpose
NOT to just take up space.

# Chapter 15

## *Birth Out Of Darkness*

Why do I feel like breaking out in a praise dance or running right about now?

It's because I realize just how much God's hands are in and over my life. I am both excited and emotional about my journey. I thank God I don't look like what I've been through, and I'm amazed that I'm still here. I'm still here closed in my right mind. I'm not incarcerated or in a mental ward. I didn't succeed in my attempt to take my own life, and I didn't take matters into my own hands and killed somebody for what they did to me.

I couldn't put every single shifting moment of my life into one book because there would not be enough pages. I provided significant moments that I know I had God's blessing and covering over me. I pray that my story will help you to understand that life can be born out of the darkness.

My birthing place started as a result of words spoken into a little girl's life at seven years old: Words intended to keep her in the dark. Little did they know that she would use those words as a means of guiding her back towards God's light. When that didn't work, the enemy attempted to rip her innocence away from her through rape, but God took her to a place of darkness for her to survive the trauma. The night gave her a place of protection until she was strong enough to face what had happened to her. The darkness of shame was cast on her as a teenage mother, but the joy and light of her newborn son brought her new meaning and purpose. His love and the responsibility God had given her pushed her closer to the SON (Jesus Christ). Then the enemy attempted to beat the remaining light out of her to the point of her wanting to stay in darkness because the abuse almost cost her everything.

If beating her was not enough, he snatched her heart out of her when the affair took place, making her feel like it was pointless to love or live. Oh, but the passion was restored by a second son that healed her broken heart while making her believe in love again. As she fought her way back from the darkness, her place of peace and safety was gone with the loss of her father while she struggled to find her place in the heart of her mother. As the darkness of depression slowly moved in, she was losing her will to fight and almost gave in to the darkness again.

God helped her to realize that the darkness was only her traveling through the birth canal. The pain and trauma were only contractions to indicate that birth was taking place. The brokenness in ministry was her water breaking, letting her know to not give up but to keep pushing. Therapy placed her feet in the stirrups. The shaving of her head was the baby's crowning. The day she released all her little girls, the shoulders were popping out. The baby finally came into this new world, and she gave birth to a women's ministry, a talk show, a blog, a podcast, and poetry.

The birthing of this book allowed me to see what God has been doing all this time finally birthing me out of the darkness. He was creating a Phoenix to rise out of the ashes.

May you birth something out of this season. I hope my words inspire you to tell your story without fear or apprehension. I pray that your bravery and courage sprays a beam of light on every single inch of darkness attempting to hold you back.

Always Remember…

- We have to be careful about being silent while we're going through. Don't get me wrong there is a time to be silent so you can clearly hear from Him but never lose your sensitivity in the spirit. Someone is always in need of thee…your wisdom, your testimony, your encouragement and your calling. Lord give me the wisdom and the sensitivity to know when to speak and when to be silent but most of all teach me how to always be available for when you have a need for me!

- Let your light shine so when you encounter someone in darkness they can have a safe place to land. When you are in your right place with God there's no way you'll intentionally let anyone crash when they're trying to land.

- Life can grow out of darkness especially when you let the light in.

- Allow your trauma to take you from pain to power.

- If I can birth something out of my dark place, so can you.

God,

    Thank you for choosing me for such a time as this. Thank you for taking my dark experiences and birthing ministry.

    God, thank you that everything that happens to us and through us can be utilized to bring souls closer to you. Thank you for protecting my spirit, my mind and my soul during my traumatic experiences.

    God, I ask that you touch each person individually and let them know that darkness is a birthing place and that what didn't kill you can be used to destroy the enemy assigned to us. I encourage each of you to embrace your story and declare victory over everything assigned to you.

In Jesus' Name,

Amen

Bertrille Williams

# *For You*

## *My Beauty*

My beauty is not defined by the length of my hair or the features on my face.

It's not based upon my pant size, shoe size, or if I'm snatched around my waist.

It's not based upon the width of my chest or the size of my behind. But based upon how I use my brain, not my body, what comes out of my mouth, the value I place upon myself and what goes on inside my brilliant mind.

It's not based upon a man, the pack I run with, or a brand of makeup. But it's based upon how many lives I impact, the love I give to others, and how we lift each other up.

We've got this whole thing twisted because a figure and good looks can fade.

It's all about how you walk this thing called life out while setting the world ablaze.

I must constantly remind myself to see the beauty that's within me.

A strong, confident woman who is totally beautiful in the skin you see.

## Bertrille Williams

If I could leave you with a hashtag, what exactly would it be?

#Bald,
#Bold
#Beautiful
#PhenomenallyMe!

## *Don't Come For Me!*

So, because I'm bald, you thought you could come for me when I didn't send for you.

You see, what you failed to realize is my baldness has nothing to do with you, Boo Boo! All you are is an Internet troll.

With no life, no ambitions, no clue, and no goals. You hide behind your mean comments, bullying anyone you can. But let's keep it real we all know it's you with the problems, low self-esteem, and no man.

My baldness is bold, beautiful, and totally me. Because I learned one of the secrets to life, it's okay to be me and totally free.

Love yourself, be kind to others, and never let anyone tell you who or what you can be.

My hair does not define me, nor will the lack of it keep me in bondage.

So, your words mean nothing to me because, unlike you, I'm no longer damaged.

Let me leave you with this one last thing like the song by India Arie "I am not my hair!" so think twice about the next time you try to come

Bertrille Williams

for me!

# The Quarantine Talent Show

Lord, I just want to thank you for allowing me to be a part of the quarantine talent show.

You gave this vision to a man with humility, a heart for people, a brilliant sense of humor, and we thank you for blessing this world with Comic Steve Brown, our most gifted host.

He understands that this is a Kingdom assignment, and it's not about how many viewers, followers, likes, or hearts he can get.

But it's about allowing people to share their talents with the world by expressing themselves and giving the quarantine talent show audience their best.

It may have started as entertainment, a way to help us get through this quarantine.

Then God decided to make it more significant than just a platform for spoken word, jokes, and a method for an artist to show how well they can sing.

We became a great big family by praying for each other and pushing each other through.

We helped each other through depression, sickness, divorce, death, and dating, just to name a few.

We learn to support each other and discover that there's more to life than just thinking it's all about you.

The quarantine may be coming to an end as we transition back to our regular lives and jobs.

Comic Steven Steve Brown, I don't think you realize what kind of impact your obedience has caused.

You challenged people to face their fears, get over their insecurities, created a family atmosphere, and helped people to live out their dreams.

You opened up our hearts and eyes while making us realize we can accomplish anything.

Just know that God is pleased by what you are doing, and because of your obedience, our lives will never be the same because you allowed God to use you to be a blessing to us with the quarantine talent show.

God is going to make sure the whole world is about to know your name.

For my new quarantine talent show family, I

don't have to call any names because you know who you are.

May God continue to open up the doors of favor in each of your lives because he created you all to be his superstars.

Bertrille Williams

## *Black Man Swag*

I was inspired to celebrate and recognize our African, black Kings.

The man that carries the seed of life. Who is our hero, provider, protector, our strength, and our everything.

Swagger is defined as someone who walks with an expression of attitude, confidence, style, and grace.

This man knows exactly who he is, and he doesn't mind letting you know by the expression of boldness and gratitude written all over his face.

Can't nobody carry himself like a King or walk this Earth as a black man can.

You can feel the power in every step he takes, see elegance in the way he dresses, and he doesn't expect anyone to compliment him or tell him he's the man.

He was created as a Masterpiece, chiseled by the Gods, from the soles of his feet to the tips of his strong but gentle hands.

He has no problem at all with doing whatever

it takes to care and provide for his family in any way he can.

God made him in all shades of darkness; everybody type you can imagine. He made him brilliant, loving, and kind.

Despite all that, he has been through and sacrificed. God made him withstand adversity and the test of time.

Don't believe what they say about him. They are not all criminals, thugs, dead beats, cheaters that's further from the truth.

They are fathers, husbands, hard workers, and can take over this world when a strong woman motivates him and decides to turn him loose.

So Black man swag shows the world what you're made of.

Strength, Power, confidence, wisdom, and God's perfect LOVE.

## *You Got My Back?*

You say you are my brother's and my sister's keeper, so why aren't you giving me a hand?

Why aren't you speaking your truth or sharing your wisdom with me about how you were able to overcome life's most challenging demands.

Revelations 12:11 decrees, "And they overcame him by the blood of the lamb and by the word of their testimony."

Yet we are afraid to strip down naked in transparency.

Instead, we go silent and pretend like there's nothing wrong with me.

See, it's the unspoken words that are killing us, that secret life we are trying to live.

It's not until God pulls the covers off of us, exposing us and letting the whole world know, "Hey, this thing just got real!"

It's not about me trying to get all up in your business; man it's greater than all of that. It's about letting you stand on my shoulders until you can recover from what landed you on your back.

I'm not trying to compete with you, complete you, or even become you.

I'm just trying to be there when you need me because that's what a real ride or die, sister, brother, or friend will do.

So, if you need a helping hand when someone tries to come for you, together with prayer, we can bust the enemy down to the white meat. Because the mighty God that we serve is the heavyweight champion of the world with nothing but wins and zero defeats, so, the next time you see me falling, please don't talk about me.

Just extend me a helping hand and say, "come on, get up, we got this and let me show you how to get free."

Thank you for all the times you've had my back and been there for me. Because without your love and support, I don't know where I would be.

## *Do You See?*
### *(Dedicated to Comedian Shaky)*

Shout out to my man Shaky, one of my number one comedians or at least one of my top five. I admire your passion, your humor, your fight, and you make me feel grateful just to be alive.

When I see you, my focus is not on your disabilities, but I see you as handi-capable.

Capable of overcoming adversity, capable of living your best life, capable of speaking your whole truth, capable of telling the world I am higher than all of your negative labels.

So, when you see me know that you are looking at a blessed man.

A man of strength, power, confidence, and the ability to do anything that you can.

Although you see me laughing on the outside, you have no idea what my inner struggles are or how I feel.

How my challenges, my frustrations, and how people try to remind me that my disability is real?

So, when you come across someone who is

handi-capable. Don't point your fingers, don't stare at them or treat them differently.

They are human beings, believe it or not; they are just like you and me. They are trying to figure out who or what they would like to be.

It doesn't matter if you were born that way or as a result of a tragedy. God saw fit to keep you here because he has need for thee.

Shaky, in the beginning, I asked the question, do you see me? The answer is yes; I see your joy, your pain, your wisdom, and the favor of God upon your life as you walk in total victory.

## Get Connected with Author Bertrille Williams on Social Media

 @ WilliamsBertrille

 @ favored4this

# Birth Out of Darkness

www.ingramcontent.com/pod-product-compliance
Lightning Source LLC
Chambersburg PA
CBHW061200070526
44579CB00009B/79